Wish Granted

25 Stories of Strength and Resilience
from America's Favorite Athletes

BY MAKE-A-WISH® WITH DON YAEGER

with an introduction by Chief Wish Ambassador
Michael Jordan

MAKE·Ⓐ·WISH®

HarperOne
An Imprint of HarperCollinsPublishers

HarperOne

WISH GRANTED: *25 Stories of Strength and Resilience from America's Favorite Athletes.* Copyright © 2014 by Make-A-Wish Foundation of America. All rights reserved. Printed in the United States of America. No part of this book may be used or reproduced in any manner whatsoever without written permission except in the case of brief quotations embodied in critical articles and reviews. For information address HarperCollins Publishers, 195 Broadway, New York, NY 10007.

HarperCollins books may be purchased for educational, business, or sales promotional use. For information please e-mail the Special Markets Department at SPsales@harpercollins.com.

HarperCollins website: http://www.harpercollins.com

HarperCollins®, ▲®, and HarperOne™ are trademarks of HarperCollins Publishers.

Make-A-Wish website: http://wish.org

Make-A-Wish Foundation®, Make-A-Wish®, Celebration of Wishes℠, Delicious Wishes℠, Season of Wishes®, Serving Up Wishes℠, Stories of Light®, Summer of Wishes℠, and the Make-A-Wish swirl-and-star logo are marks of the Make-A-Wish Foundation of America. All other marks are the property of their respective owners.

FIRST EDITION

Designed by Terry McGrath

The credits on page 209 constitute a continuation of this copyright page.

Library of Congress Cataloging-in-Publication Data

Make-A-Wish Foundation.
   Wish granted : 25 stories of strength and resilience from America's favorite athletes / Make-A-Wish Foundation.
       pages cm.
   ISBN 978–0–06–221839–1
   1. Athletes—United States—Conduct of life. 2. Athletes—United States—Psychology.
3. Make-A-Wish Foundation. I. Title.
GV706.55.M34 2014
796.01—dc23   2013041008

14 15 16 17 18 RRD(H) 10 9 8 7 6 5 4 3 2 1

Wish Granted is dedicated to all the heroes—athletes, celebrities, and other extraordinary people—who have helped Make-A-Wish grant hundreds of thousands of life-changing wishes. By granting wishes, you have influenced the lives and health of thousands of wish kids around the world—the true impact of your compassion and generosity is immeasurable. These wishes have captured the world, inspired communities, and most importantly instilled hope and joy in children and families when they needed it most.

We are forever grateful.

Contents

CONTENTS

Wish Granted

Michael Jordan

*Every year in the United States alone, approximately
twenty-seven thousand children are diagnosed with a life-threatening
medical condition. Twenty-seven thousand. It breaks your heart, doesn't it?*

I've worn a lot of hats in my day, but the one that I think I might be most proud of is Chief Wish Ambassador for Make-A-Wish. Each year, the foundation grants wishes for roughly 14,000 seriously ill children—a number that has been increasing every year since 1980. Next year, I'm sure the number will be even higher. It's a wonderful record to continue breaking because it means we are reaching more and more kids, but it's also a terrible number because it means that children continue to get sick.

I've always had a soft spot for kids' charities. For years I have partnered with groups like Make-A-Wish, Special Olympics, and Ronald McDonald House because it means the world to me that children and families with special needs and facing such big challenges might get even a little encouragement from my involvement. That's an incredible and humbling feeling.

It's tough sometimes as an athlete to decide to which charities you should dedicate your time and influence, because the need is so great and there are so many

wonderful causes out there. One of the many reasons that Make-A-Wish in particular is so near to my heart is that they aren't "specialized" in terms of who they serve; in other words, a three-year-old with a congenital heart condition is as much a part of their demographic as is a sixteen-year-old battling leukemia. They don't focus on just one type of disease or one specific age group. Their goal is to grant wishes to as many seriously ill children as possible. Period.

That's a pretty tall—and pretty amazing—order. Those of us who have the honor of getting to participate in granting those wishes are a very lucky group. Just the knowledge that a child's one wish, more than anything else in the world, is to meet you—that is better than anything else you can accomplish in life: better than any athletic accolade you might receive or award you might be given or record you might set. It means that you have earned someone's respect to such a degree that a visit from you, a chat, maybe a photograph, is something that inspires them so much they want to keep fighting whatever life-threatening condition might be plaguing them. It gives me goose bumps just thinking about it.

I've been privileged enough over the last two decades to be a part of two hundred wishes, and I'm not exaggerating when I say that each one was special to me in its own way. It's hard to pick out one particular wish that stands out, since that's almost like asking a parent to pick their favorite child, but I do remember one young woman named Katie back in 2002, who had been diagnosed with malignant tumors in her brain. I happened to be granting wishes in Washington D.C. that year and was visiting with a roomful of wish kids and their families. Everyone had basketballs they

wanted signed, or maybe some shoes. Each family was seated at their own table, and after talking to the room as a whole, I went from table to table to talk with each kid and their siblings and parents individually and take some photos. When I got to Katie's table, her family was obviously very excited to see me,  but she seemed a little shy and tongue-tied. I wanted to make sure that she got the special experience she was hoping for. This was her wish, after all, so after talking a bit with her family, I turned to Katie and asked her, "Is there anything you want?" She just looked up at me and squeaked out, "Can I have a hug?"

Something inside me absolutely melted at those words. Here is this sweet kid who has been through so much, and all she wants from me is a hug! It was awesome. She was crying, her parents were crying, and I choked up, too. In that one moment, I was reminded exactly why it is that I want to work with Make-A-Wish. *That's* what it's all about.

But that's not the end of Katie's story. A few years ago, I learned that she not only triumphed over her illness, she is now grown up and, for a while, worked for Make-A-Wish. It was awesome to learn about her life over the past ten years, to hear

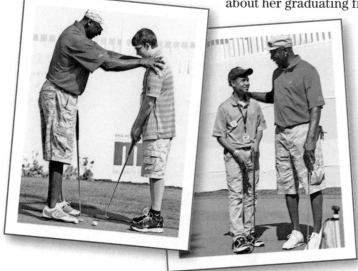

about her graduating from school and going on to college and how her illness will always be something she has to be aware of but that is not front and center in her life anymore. Having her wish granted meant so much to her that she was determined to someday help make wishes come true for other children, which meant that she had to first overcome her cancer. The best parallel I can make to my own life was my desire to have a Hall of Fame career. I was so set on reaching that goal that I was motivated to practice longer and work harder than anyone else so that I would have a shot. Finding out that a wish in which I had a part inspired that same kind of drive, except with infinitely higher stakes, was pretty incredible.

Because that's what Make-A-Wish does: they don't just grant a wish; they empower with hope.

There was a study released recently that found that 81 percent of parents and 58 percent of healthcare professionals noticed an increased willingness of children to undergo difficult treatments once they participated in Make-A-Wish. The kids wanted to feel good enough to enjoy their wishes, and they also came back from them with a more positive and empowered mind-set. After all, they had just asked for something that came true; for many kids, that's the first time they've felt any control or power over their lives after months or maybe even years of treatments. In fact, 74 percent of parents said that when their child's wish was granted, it marked a turning point in the treatment process. Those are significant numbers!

I'd like to share another story of a young lady named Carmen whom I met working with another great group, Special Olympics. She had a condition that caused her to be in a wheelchair, and her life expectancy was only about fifteen years. She was a huge Bulls fan, and after we met through Special Olympics when she was eleven or twelve, I made sure she had season tickets to go to all our games. Now, almost fifteen years later, she defied all the odds not only by surviving to the age of twenty-seven, but thriving. She lives in Chicago where she has a job, is married, and has a healthy baby. It's absolutely amazing. Kids like Katie and Carmen are such a wonderful testament to the power of positive thinking and to the indomitability of the human spirit.

Of course, not all stories end that happily. One of the hardest things to face with organizations like Make-A-Wish is that not all of the kids with whom you get to build relationships are going to make it. Some pass away not long after you get to meet them; others combat their illnesses for years, sometimes even going into remission, before they finally lose the fight. Whenever I get word that one of "my" kids is gone, it hurts because, as anyone who has ever granted a wish will tell you, you really do forge a bond with them. You've become part of their experience, just as they've become a part

of your life. You were rooting for them to win just as much as they have ever cheered for you during one of your games.

Growing up is tough enough without hospital stays and clinic visits, chemotherapy or radiation treatment, open-heart surgery, transplant lists, or whatever else the children that Make-A-Wish helps have to face. Some of them have birthday parties in their hospital room where most of the guests are nurses and doctors. Some of them have lost their hair or are now marked with large scars. Some are able to go to school but have to take extra precautions in everything they do instead of being able to just run around and enjoy a carefree childhood. The thing that unites all of these children is that they just want to feel normal.

Something I have learned from all my years of working with kids is that every kid—no matter who they are or what they are dealing with—wants to feel normal. So whenever I grant a wish, that's exactly what I try to give them. I try to make it feel like a casual time, like we're just a couple of old friends hanging out. For so many of these kids, everything has been a big deal or high drama for a very long time. They don't really get a chance to feel like there isn't a heavy weight on their shoulders, and the last thing I want to do is add to their stress (or to the stress of their families) by making them feel starstruck or like they have to make a big deal out of the visit. I just want them to feel like they are a normal kid and a normal family with a normal life for one day, and they just happen to be spending some time with a really tall, goofy guy from Chicago by way of North Carolina.

It's funny how many kids still ask to meet me; you'd think that they'd want to meet an active player instead of some old retired guy, but the wishes keep coming, and I'll keep granting them as long as they do. I usually grant two wishes a year these days: one in Charlotte, North Carolina, and one in Chicago. Each group has about six kids who have flown in from all around the country, and we spend the day as a group, making friends with one another and playing around. But after nearly two decades of meeting with Make-A-Wish children, I have come to know what to expect when I first arrive. For whatever reason, the number one question every kid seems to ask when we first meet is about the number of cars that I have. So now I've worked out a system where, before I even sit down with them, I introduce myself and say, "What are your names? Where are you from? Where do you all know me from because I know it can't be basketball—you're not that old. It was from *Space Jam*, right?" That gets them laughing.

Then I add one more thing to my introduction: "Let me start by answering all the questions that everyone wants to know. I have X number of cars. I only have one house. My kids are such and such. I started playing basketball when I was twelve.

Now, let's go with all the *different* questions!" That usually gets the kids laughing even harder, as if I read their minds, and then we start talking about some of the more unique issues they want to ask about . . . like what it was like hanging out with Bugs Bunny on the set of *Space Jam*. In fact, it's funny how few of the kids want to talk much about basketball at all. We might chat a bit about the Knicks if they're from New York or the Jazz if they're from Utah or talk college hoops if they have a favorite team. Of course, there are always some who want to talk hoops or about my line of shoes, and that's great, too—I'm there for whatever they want. But most kids just want to get to know *me* and aren't all that concerned about my career. And I love that because I'm there to talk about whatever they want and to celebrate them. I want them to tell me about themselves, to introduce me to their families, to talk about their illness if they want to or talk about something else entirely if they don't. It's their day. I'll sign whatever they want me to sign, take whatever pictures they want to take, and just make them feel special—normal and special.

In January 2009, when Make-A-Wish named me the Chief Wish Ambassador, I was incredibly honored. It was really an awesome feeling to know that a group like that felt I could help raise awareness and support for their work. What a wonderful gift! But really, every encounter with a wish child is a gift of some form. Even now, as I grant my two hundredth wish, it's still as exciting for me as the very first time I ever granted one. Every wish keeps me humble as I look around and see the pain and challenges that other people face in their lives. It's easy for most of us to see hurting people in newspapers or on TV suffering and to sometimes forget that they have real emotions in their lives beyond those pictures: sadness, confusion, frustration, despair, hopelessness, depression . . . but also happiness, hopefulness, determination, and defiance.

By purchasing this book, you, too, are helping to grant wishes, as the money earned will go directly to Make-A-Wish to help grow and continue its work.

So, thank you.

Thank you for caring enough to pick up this book and consider the stories about lives that have been impacted through the work of Make-A-Wish—not just the children's lives, but the athletes, too. And thank you for what your purchase will mean to thousands of seriously ill children whose wishes you will help come true. Those kids are my heroes, and by actively deciding to help them continue their fight with a little more hope, you're one of my heroes, too.

SEEING DREAMS AND WISHES
COMING TRUE

Michael Phelps

Now that my Olympic career is behind me, I can look at my

twenty-two medals and think, "That was pretty amazing—a dream come true."

But outside of the medals, I can say without a doubt that my favorite thing about

my career has been the opportunity it has given me to get involved in granting

wishes for the incredible kids who are part of Make-A-Wish. I honestly mean

that, because of the tremendous impact those kids have had on my perspective,

my understanding of real strength, and on how I want to live my life.

It's hard to put into words the feeling you get when you see a child's face light up with a huge grin when they realize you're there just for them. It is such an honor to be able to meet someone who is so brave and so strong and who says that they've been influenced or encouraged by you. That is an incredible, inspiring moment that will never get old or less special, no matter how many times I get to experience it. It's a chance to really feel like you are touching the hearts of not only sick children, but their families, too. Where else do you get a chance to do something that significant?

But even more than that, it's so exciting to get to stay connected with the kids long after their wish is over—to get to see how they are growing, to hear about their various milestones, to cheer them on as they continue their fight to defeat their disease or condition every day of their life, and in some cases, to see them leave that difficult chapter of their lives behind them as they go on to enjoy healthy and whole lives, chasing after their own dreams.

I truly believe in the power of wishes to encourage people to keep fighting their diagnoses because I have seen in my own family how a wish can make a difference. My grandmother has always been an extremely important figure in my life, so when she was diagnosed with cancer and given only a few months to live, I was completely heartbroken. But my grandma had a wish to see me compete in the 2004 Olympics, so she held on until that wish came true, outliving the doctors' predictions. Having a goal became her motivation to keep fighting her cancer just a little longer. She knew she had to leave this life, but she was going to do it on her terms, having achieved something she desperately wanted first. Make-A-Wish does the same thing for kids, providing them with something exciting to look forward to, which then motivates them not to lose heart but to keep fighting for as long as possible. It gives them the opportunity to tell their disease or condition, "You don't win until I've had my say." That's powerful. I was so happy that I could give that Olympic dream to my grandma, and I am so humbled that my career has also allowed me to share that gift with others.

I've had the privilege of being a part of a lot of wishes over the past few years, and each one has shown me how important the foundation's work is. Some of "my" wish kids have been fighting life-threatening illnesses; others have genetic conditions that severely limit their lives and make every day a struggle. And with every child, I have had a chance to meet a new family, learn about their story, and see their courage. I can't tell you how significant that is—not only to hear what they're going through but also to see how they are standing up under the stress, sadness, and uncertainty. Getting to know even one of those families would be life-changing in itself, but I've had the honor of meeting close to a dozen of them.

I really look forward to those wishes. In fact (and this is terrible to admit), I'll sometimes see stuff on my schedule and kind of be like, "Eh, whatever." I'll brush it off or just ignore it if it doesn't interest me until my scheduler has to get on my case about it. But any time Make-A-Wish shows up, I call back right away to say I'm in. There is no putting it off or weighing my options. When I learn that there is a child who wants to meet me, I want to get the ball rolling immediately. The wishes really do have that kind of an impact on *everyone* involved. The children and their families may be excited, but I promise you that I am, too!

I try to make sure that the whole experience is very relaxed for everyone. I remember when I got to meet Michael Jordan, my number one sports icon. I just froze. I couldn't think of anything to say. I couldn't think of anything I wanted to ask him. My mind just went blank. Eventually, he got me to relax, and it ended up being an incredible moment, but it was also kind of terrifying at first. Every time I get ready to meet a wish kid, I think of that experience and I want to make sure that no one feels speechless like I did. Thankfully, all the wish kids I've met have been a lot cooler meeting me than I was meeting Jordan. We usually sit around for a bit and get to know each other, telling stories and asking questions. The first one everyone asks is, "How does it feel to win an Olympic gold medal?" I answer them as honestly as possible: "It's a dream come true." Then, depending on the child's health and wish, either they'll watch me practice and train in order to learn what it's like "behind the scenes" of an Olympic workout, or we'll jump in the pool together and just swim and play for a while. Afterward, we'll have a meal together. It's nothing formal or fancy— just a fun day of making new friends and spending some time together in a way that lets the child know they are special and important.

I explain to the kids that it doesn't matter how hard you have to work or how long you have to train: if you're determined to do something, no one will be able to stop you as long as you refuse to let them. That's what got me to the Olympics. A lot of people don't realize just how powerful mental toughness really is—it's every bit as important in competition as muscles and technique. My body isn't a typical swimmer's body; instead of long legs, I have short legs and a long torso. I heard more than once that I probably wouldn't have much of a career in swimming because of that. But I refused to accept those limitations, which just goes to show what the mind can do if you have the discipline and determination to make your dream happen.

At the same time, I feel a little silly talking to these kids about overcoming obstacles. I mean, I've had my share of injuries and challenges, and my career has had its ups and downs, but I've experienced nothing—*nothing*—like what these kids are facing on a daily basis. I draw so much inspiration from them, watching how they've tackled their own situations with so much heart and passion, refusing to let their condition win, even if that means holding it off for just one more day. My mom sometimes helps out with various wishes, and she and I always discuss them afterward. More than once I have remarked to her, "Nothing I've gone through even compares to what those kids have gone through." I am so incredibly lucky to be twenty-eight and have accomplished everything I've wanted to . . . but it's never been anything as important or as tough as fighting for my life. Those wish kids are my heroes, and I never would have gotten the chance to meet them if it weren't for Make-A-Wish.

There are so many stories I could tell about the amazing people I've gotten to meet through the foundation and other philanthropic work, but there is one child whom I got to know very early on, and our time together will always stand out to me as the one that introduced me to the joy of interacting with seriously ill children and inspired me to make that a real goal of my career.

I was still living and training up in Michigan, where I'm from, and a boy named Stevie who was from the same area had asked to meet me. Stevie was battling brain cancer but was staying active and competing with his swim team even as he was combating the disease. After I met him that first time, I knew that just one day wasn't enough. He was such a neat, dynamic kid, and I wanted to stay a part of his life. Since he didn't live too far away, his parents would invite me over to their house to shoot hoops or kick around a soccer ball in the yard. I'd sit with his parents and sister at Stevie's swim meets to cheer him on. Our families became close friends as he and I encouraged each other to keep chasing our dreams.

Stevie's health seemed to go up and down a lot as his cancer responded to, and then resisted, treatment. I had seen all that my grandmother had gone through with

her own fight against cancer, so I knew how uncertain things can be, how some days things look so hopeful, and how hard it can be when there is no more hope for recovery and all you can do is wait for the end and pray it is peaceful.

I was lucky enough to get to walk beside Stevie for that last part of his fight, and to be with him just a few days before he died. He had gone home from the hospital and had reached a point where he couldn't really react to anyone or anything. I just sat there with him in his room, holding his hand, talking to him, and praying for him for a long time. My mom joined us after a while, and the three of us sat there while my mom and I recalled memories we'd all had together of swimming or playing basketball or just hanging out with our families. Eventually, his parents and sister came in, too, and we all just sat there talking about what an amazing kid Stevie was and how much he had touched our lives. I feel absolutely certain that somehow, even though he couldn't respond, he heard every word we said and was enjoying the memories along with us. He died just a few days later at the age of twelve.

I was in college at the time and missed my classes in order to attend his funeral. I was doing okay until I saw that, among the photos the family had displayed to celebrate Stevie's life, there were several pictures of us together from our wish day as well as other times afterward that we spent together. It was such a moving experience to see how much those interactions had meant to Stevie and his family, how just a few hours of my time here and there had cheered them up so much. I'm not sure if Stevie ever knew how much encouragement he offered me in return. Just sitting there, looking at those images of a little boy going through so much pain—it was hard to fathom why that had to happen, especially to a family so kind and loving. But seeing those photos also reminded me that my work for Stevie wasn't done; I could stand by his parents and sister while they grieved. Of course, there was nothing I could do to fix the situation, nothing anyone could do to make everything better. Just walking alongside someone who is mourning, however, listening to them talk and letting them know you care, can be the most important thing anyone can offer.

Stevie's family is still close with mine. They have come to a number of my swim meets and always have big hugs for me afterward. We still sometimes talk about what an amazing person their son was and how incredible it is that a twelve-year-old boy could have such a lasting and profound impact on the adults in his life.

A lot of people don't know this about me, but I am very into journaling. I am constantly writing about my life, my thoughts, my emotions, my goals. Sometimes I still find myself journaling about my grandmother and about Stevie. I hate that I had to lose them both to cancer, but I also find comfort in knowing that they are looking down on me, supporting me, and cheering me on with every decision I have to make. It's such a great feeling knowing that there are some relationships and some friendships that are so powerful that death doesn't end them. It's true that if I'd never met Stevie and his family, I wouldn't have had to deal with the sadness of watching his struggle and his death, but without him I also wouldn't have had the opportunity to learn so much about true strength, true courage, and truly living life to the fullest to make the most of whatever time you have left.

At a dinner in Chicago a while back, someone told me that they had heard the story about my friendship with Stevie and asked me what it was like. We both got emotional as I described our friendship, as well as the difference in my life that *all* those special interactions have made. Every single one of those kids has made a real difference to me.

If someone were to ask me to explain why wish granting is so important, I think the best way to explain it would be like this: my favorite part of swimming is being a part of relay teams because, while the individual events are exciting, they are also just me competing alone against everyone else in the pool. Relay events give me a chance to be a part of something bigger, competing *with* people instead of only against them. You have to rely on everybody to come together in order for your team to be successful. We are more powerful with more people, and it's amazing to see a number of individuals work together toward the exact same goal. I couldn't have asked for a better way for my Olympic career to have ended than with a relay race in which we won the gold.

Being part of the Make-A-Wish team gives me that same feeling. I get to be part of a much bigger team that is working together to help out children going through something tougher than most of us can possibly imagine. But unlike the Olympics, I don't have any plans to retire from working with Make-A-Wish. I would

love to do more events, grant more wishes, and be a part of that team for as long as there is a need. I've been lucky enough to have my professional dreams come true; what better way to share that joy than to help sick children see their own wishes become reality?

YOU CAN'T SAY NO

Ken Griffey, Jr.

Honestly, it is really scary when you learn that a seriously ill

child has requested to meet you, out of anything they could have picked to

do. For someone to think so highly of what you do that his or her wish is

to spend the day with you—it's just incredible. You cannot turn that down.

You just can't. No matter what else is on your schedule, you just have to

make it work. You also immediately start to worry if you will be able to live

up to their expectations and make the big day be everything they hope it

will be. Can you possibly do enough to be worthy of being their wish?

There are a couple of rules that I follow whenever I have the opportunity to meet with a wish child. First and foremost, I tell the child that the wish is not about me or any other athlete. Even though we were the ones who have been "chosen," the focus on the day should not be that they get to meet us but that we get the opportunity to make our time together all about them. I tell the parents, "This is about your son or daughter and whatever they want to do. I'll give them the whole major league experience, if they want. Please assure your child that they don't need to be nervous about talking to me. I am there for them."

The second thing I do is to tell the child that the only thing he or she can't take is my glove. Everything else is theirs for the asking. Do they want a bat? Here you go. Do they want my jersey? Take it. My cleats or a batting glove or my cap? Done. Not a problem. It can all be replaced. There have been years when I have gone through ten or fifteen jerseys because several wish children asked for one.

I first started working with Make-A-Wish after a friend told me about them. I volunteer with several organizations geared toward helping children, but Make-A-Wish is unique in what it does. I read one story recently in which a teenage girl's wish was to go to her high school prom, but she couldn't leave her hospital room. So what did Make-A-Wish do? They had a prom for her *in* her hospital room. That's just amazing. I get emotional just thinking about all the people who came together to make that happen for her. That kind of thing matters to the kids who are fighting their various conditions and to the families who are fighting alongside them. Kids are the future. They are going to be running the country someday, and they deserve to have happiness and support. In the long run, no one is going to care about what I do; what they will care about are the experiences that shaped the lives of tomorrow's leaders. What we do today to reach out to children and their families matters in the long run. It really does.

I am always a little concerned, though, that the child will be too overwhelmed to really enjoy the wish. Sometimes, kids get timid or shy when they meet someone they've only ever seen on TV, so getting off a little bit away from the crowd so that we can interact one-on-one often helps them loosen up and feel more comfortable.

Whatever they want to do is what we'll do. If they want to hit baseballs, we'll go to the batting cage. If they want to play catch, we'll throw the ball as long as they want. If they want to be part of the team, I might even be able to include them in our pregame meeting. I've done that with several wish kids, and they've always loved the behind-the-scenes look at a real team getting ready to play. If they want to field some

balls, I'll send them to the outfield and step up to the plate to hit to them. If some of my teammates are out there with the child on the field, I'll always tell them, "You protect this kid—got it?" And they always do. Everyone wants to look out for the kid and make their day as exciting and as perfect as can be. Sometimes it's hard to tell who's having more fun—us or them.

I hope parents understand that as they watch professional athletes interact with children during a wish. The experience brings us joy. It really does. It reminds us that we aren't playing ball because ball games really matter all that much—we are doing it because it provides people with something to root for, to get excited about, to help them forget their troubles for a little while. Meeting with wish children puts it all into perspective: our game matters only as much as it matters to the fans, and those kids are our most important ones.

That's why I will never turn a wish down. For several years, I had ten or more wish requests each season, and I was always so excited to be a part of each of those. Now, even though I'm retired, if Make-A-Wish called me and said, "We have a kid who needs to come tomorrow," I would say, "Okay. You got it." If I have to move some things around on my schedule or rearrange some personal time, so be it. If it's in my power to make it happen, I will, and I know I'm not alone. There are plenty of other athletes who feel the same way and have done the same thing. Sometimes you have the flexibility to wait a bit and make sure all the arrangements are in place. But sometimes you don't.

The first child for whom I ever granted a wish was a seven-year-old boy. As we were talking about baseball and my family and everything except his disease (he had no interest in discussing that), it became clear that he would love to have a jersey. The only problem was that I didn't have one on hand because it wasn't a game day.

So I jumped in my car, raced home, got him one, and brought it back. The look on his face was absolutely priceless. He couldn't believe that I would do that for him, but I told him, "Look—a jersey's just a jersey." My jersey isn't one-of-a-kind. A person is.

That boy passed away not long after his wish, and his parents buried him wearing my jersey. I found out after a game in Philly, when I had hit a home run. I just sat in the locker room, absolutely numb. That home run, even though I hadn't realized it at the time, had been for him.

The only other time I think I have been at such a loss for words was just after 9/11, when I met a fireman before a game and he said, "Everyone always wants something *from* you. Well, here's something *for* you." And he handed me a shirt with his station's number on it. I was so humbled and amazed by that gesture, and it made me think about all my wish kids and how special that sense of a stranger genuinely caring about you really is.

I've been so lucky to meet all of the kids I have through Make-A-Wish. I remember one eight-year-old boy named C.J. who had lymphoma. It was 1994, and I had been working on my video game, so the game company coordinated the release of it with C.J.'s visit. He and I were able to sit down and play the game together—on the stadium's large-screen TV! I don't know who was more excited about that—him or me. We really battled it out with the game, and I did not hold back just because he was a kid. I ended up winning, but only by one point. C.J. did an outstanding job giving me a run for my money on a game he'd never played before! I can't even begin to express what an incredible gift he gave me by helping my game debut in such a neat way. It was such a cool day that only got cooler when I hit a home run. I was even able to get the ball back so I could give it to C.J. as he sat with his family in the stands.

Another great wish was in 1996, when there was a twelve-year-old boy named Michael who wanted to be an athlete until a diagnosis of Hodgkin's lymphoma put

all his dreams on hold. He and his family flew to Seattle to spend the day with me and go to a Mariners' game, and we had a blast. It was obvious he was a naturally gifted athlete and really mature for his age. I hate that his disease had caused him to have to stop playing. Incredibly, though, he not only beat the cancer but went on to play high school and college football, and he now coaches at the college level! He even ran in the 2013 Pittsburgh Marathon to help raise money for Make-A-Wish. That's the kind of fighting spirit these kids bring to their illnesses and conditions and their plans for the future.

That's what I mean when I say that you just can't say no. I'm sure that anyone who has spent one day with one of these incredible kids, met their families, and heard their stories cannot walk away unchanged. It's so humbling to see how just a little bit of time and effort on your part can go such a long way in lifting their spirits and giving them something to smile about in the midst of all the awfulness they're going through. You can't see that impact and not want to do it again and again.

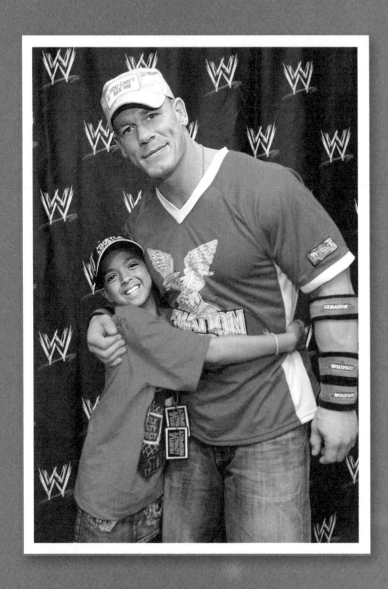

UP FOR THE FIGHT

John Cena

It's kind of difficult to talk about the work you do with a charity like Make-A-Wish without sounding self-congratulatory, but it's also difficult to raise awareness about a cause you love without talking about the work that you do. So at the risk of sounding like I am patting myself on the back, I will go ahead and state that I have granted more than three hundred wishes to date, which Make-A-Wish tells me is the highest number achieved by any individual.

But those numbers aren't about me except that they illustrate how serious I am about supporting this organization. Those numbers represent three hundred seriously ill children who have been given a special day that took them far away from the hospitals and the pain and the fear that they have to live with and has instead given them a chance to simply have fun and relish life. I can't think of a better cause to support.

When I was first starting out in wrestling back in 2002, I met a child backstage at one match who I was told was part of Make-A-Wish. I thought that was pretty cool, so I said hello and chatted with him a bit. He was there to see another wrestler, but WWE has a tradition of introducing the child to everyone when they're there for a wish in addition to spending time with the specific wrestler requested. Over the next few months, I met several kids who were there as part of Make-A-Wish. I liked getting to meet them, but I didn't really think too much about it because, embarrassingly, I hadn't heard much about Make-A-Wish and I had no idea what those visits were all about. But as I met more wish kids, I started to read more about the Make-A-Wish, and I was completely amazed by what I learned. I made two resolutions to myself: my number one goal would be to make time for every single child who came my way through Make-A-Wish, and my number two goal would be to educate people about it and the important work that it does. I didn't want anyone else to be clueless the way I was and miss out on the opportunity to do something to make these experiences as memorable and exciting for the kids as possible.

As I began to educate myself more about Make-A-Wish, my career also began to grow, so it wasn't too long before I began to get wishes from children who expressly wanted to meet me—and that was when I really started to understand how unique the wish-granting process is. That only strengthened my resolve to support Make-A-Wish however I could. There are a lot of really wonderful charities out there that bring sports figures into hospitals or use us to help raise funds for research, and that is awesome. But there's just something about the specific nature of the requests in Make-A-Wish that make a difference. The child didn't just say, "I want to meet someone famous" or "I want to hang out with a pro wrestler." Someone specifically named *you* as their wish and pinned their hopes on your time, presence, and attention. That means something.

There was one little boy in Cleveland who loved to watch wrestling and wanted to meet me, but his health was rapidly declining and the doctors said they didn't expect him to survive long. But he held on because he wanted to see his wish come true. When I learned that, I was just blown away. Immediately I told him, "We're going to get you to WrestleMania," which was happening in about six weeks. I didn't bother to check with my scheduler or agent or anyone else. I told him not to worry about the travel details, that we'd work it all out between now and then, and that his family would be my guest at that event. I can't even describe the look on his face, but it was priceless. I just wanted to give him that goal so that maybe the prospect of WrestleMania would help him hold on a little longer. He did manage to make it to the big event and he had a great time, but he passed away shortly after that.

That, to me, is what a wish can accomplish. When you're the parent of a child who is fighting an uphill battle against a disease, time becomes your most valuable asset. If the prospect of meeting someone the child watches on TV keeps him or her alive for another month, you can't put a value on that. If five airline tickets and five passes to a live event provide the hope for the child to hang on for six more weeks, it's simply not an issue of whether or not it should be done. It just needs to happen. That's the therapy of hope. Modern medicine can't objectively prove the relevance of that, but anyone who has ever seen it in action can testify to the tremendous power that it has.

After that boy passed away, his family sent me a beautiful letter, thanking me for the time and attention I'd given their son. I wrote back a sympathy card to let them know how profoundly their son had touched my own life. I wanted them to know that the experience was equally rewarding for me, and I wanted to be able to do it in a way that they would hold on to. I thought about just picking up the phone and calling them, but you can't hold a phone call in your hand years later. Handwritten letters stand the test of time, so I am a big believer in them for messages that really and truly matter—and this one did.

There was another boy who used to hang out with the 9/11 firefighters in New York. Those guys come to all of our WWE events around New York and New Jersey, and set up a tent or kiosk outside the building to help inform people about their cause. They are such a super group of guys, and they almost always had a young man with them who was engaged in a long-term fight for his life. I got to know him through his wish, and then I kept seeing him at my events when he was there with the firefighters, who had taken him under their wing. It was really cool to get to see him progress over several years, watching him grow but also seeing how happy he was, no matter what he was going through. Then, before one match, some of the firefighters told me privately that things weren't going well with his treatment. After the match, I gave that boy the shoes I had worn as sort of a unique, one-of-a-kind memento. Granted, I had lost the fight, but he didn't seem to care. He was just so appreciative about the gift that he pulled me close, looked me in the eye, and said very seriously, "Thank you. This is really, really special." Man, did I get choked up. Usually, the kids are having too much fun to stop and say thank you—and I'm totally fine with that.

That's what I want: for them to be so wrapped up in the day that they are focused only on enjoying themselves. The parents are the ones who talk to you quietly and express their thanks for giving their child and their entire family such a special experience. So for this boy to have the presence and maturity to want to give

me a genuine, heartfelt thank-you—I was just moved beyond words. All I managed to get out in response was "You're welcome. And hey—I'll see you in Trenton, okay?" Three weeks later, as I pulled up to the venue in Trenton, New Jersey, I could see that the firefighters already had their kiosk set up . . . and that the little boy wasn't there with them. I knew before they told me that he had passed away, and that was tough to take even though I had known it was coming. At moments like those, you sometimes catch yourself wondering if there was something more you could have done, something extra to make their last days as wonderful as possible. But the fact is, these kids are so grateful just for the chance to be treated like normal kids on a special day.

Watching the kids soak it all in is one of the most motivating things in the world. It's funny . . . some athletes set aside time to prepare for a wish, to get themselves into the right frame of mind, especially if the wish is taking place on a game day. For me, I find that the second someone tells me that my wish kid is on his or her way, it's

as if a switch inside me has been flipped and I'm ready to go. I've thought about trying to spend a little time prepping myself, but I've found that there is no point to it because as soon as I find out that we're about to begin, I start getting as keyed up as a little kid and can't really concentrate on anything else because I'm excited to meet the child and their family. We do the wishes in a private room at the arena so that they are able to have a unique behind-the-scenes perspective as well as have the undivided attention of my team and me despite all the hustle and bustle of the pre-event setup going on in the rest of the building. When I see them enjoying themselves like a normal family with no concerns other than just having a good time, I get a sense of "*This* is why you do what you do." It's incredibly uplifting.

Kids respond to meeting their wish granters in all sorts of ways. It's kind of difficult to predict if they are going to be talkative and boisterous or clam up and need a little coaxing to relax and see that we're just regular people. Sometimes, the kids are so geared up for the match that there is no work required to get them talking. They ask about my favorite video games or they tell me about their pets. A lot of them just say whatever comes to mind, and that always cracks me up. They are often bouncing off the walls in response to the incredible energy at the arena on an event day. It's great to watch. Other kids, though, get really quiet. I think there is a sense with them that they can't believe that this is happening. They see the superstars on TV, but they can't imagine us as real, living, breathing people. I think sometimes we're almost like superheroes to them, and it's hard to wrap your mind around someone who seems almost mythical rather than real suddenly materializing there in the room with you. In those cases, where the child seems a little overwhelmed, I just work to draw them out until, by the end of our visit, we seem like old friends. The kids with energy and not a shy bone in their bodies are always kind of a pick-me-up before matches, but the ones who are quiet are special in their own ways because there is such a sweetness to their shyness. To those kids I'll always say as I get ready to leave, "I know you're being quiet now, but you've got to promise me you'll be loud at the event!" And they always are. It's such a great feeling to look out into the crowd and see them going crazy, cheering and yelling and having a great time. The whole experience, after all, is supposed to allow them a chance to just lose themselves in the day.

I know that the time will come when kids will start making wishes to meet the next generation of wrestlers, but right now, while John Cena is still relevant, I want to do whatever I can to leverage that public attention to help seriously ill children. I have had the incredible honor of being named a Make-A-Wish ambassador, and I've spoken twice now to Make-A-Wish employees. And even though I do a good job of holding it together when I talk to families or spend time with wish kids, both times I gave speeches to the people at Make-A-Wish I almost lost it. Just looking out and seeing people who share the same ideals I have—that this is something important and we are willing to invest our time to make it happen—gets to me. One of the things I try to stress to them the most is that sometimes a job feels like a job. And while the Make-A-Wish headquarters is vibrant and alive, with the coolest pictures on the walls and a great energy about it, it's still a corporate workspace with cubicles and fluorescent lighting. But those people who fill those cubicles and work under those lights are necessary to make the charity happen. They are the ones who make everything possible. And it pays off. I've personally witnessed the happiness in the faces of kids up against incredibly tough odds; I've seen children and families absorb the positivity. It doesn't matter if you are the person who makes the coffee or the photocopies; you are a part of something great. You are creating change and doing something that puts a little more good into the world.

I know that sometimes wish kids will make a special request of an athlete to hit a home run or make a touchdown especially for them. I admire so much when the guys are able to deliver because, obviously, so many things are out of the wish kids' control. You know that they desperately want to give the kid that special moment in the game, but there are just a lot of variables that make it incredibly difficult to be able to do much more than promise to try. So when they're able to make it happen, that's just amazing to me. I'm a bit luckier in that aspect, since WWE combines sports and entertainment, because I have a little more control over some of what happens when I'm out there. Whenever I come out of the entryway before a match, I talk to the audience or to a camera, and if I have a wish kid I've been visiting with, I'm able to give him or her a direct shout-out. Also, you might notice that I always scan the crowd when I'm walking to the ring. Part of that is to just take in the audience and gauge the energy and tone, but I also try to find out ahead of time where my wish kid and their family are sitting so that I can physically acknowledge them with a wave or a point. Because the nature of our sport is such that we can modify our actions a little more than the average athletes to give the kids special moments during the competition, I think we wrestlers have a unique opportunity and responsibility to make sure that we give the kids something extra special.

That's one of the things that I'm particularly proud of: WWE has worked especially hard over the past decade or so to make sure that there is an organization-wide understanding of and appreciation for Make-A-Wish. The lack of awareness that I experienced as a young guy is no longer an issue. We've all gotten involved and invested in one way or another so that now, I honestly don't think there is a single person in all of WWE who would say no to a wish or turn down a request from Make-A-Wish. From the superstars to the managers to the divas to anyone else you can think of, we all have a shared goal of helping these kids make memories and

experience one of the greatest days of their lives. We sometimes almost compete for them. I can't tell you how many times I've seen wrestlers get introduced to their wish kids, and in taking them around to meet the other wrestlers, had guys ask, "Is there anyone for me? Do I get to grant a wish today?" We look forward to meeting these kids because they remind us why we do what we do—it's all for the fans. Their great attitudes and inspiring stories are a huge encouragement to all of us. We sometimes joke that it's become a rite of passage: when you grant your first wish for a child who specifically asked to meet you, you know you've got a career that people are paying attention to, but more importantly, you have a real, tangible fan base whom you are wrestling for.

As I said at the beginning, it's kind of tough to find the balance between getting

the word out about the great work Make-A-Wish is doing and keeping the wish a private thing that you do because it's the right thing to do, and not because you want the publicity. But when it comes down to it, the best way to make a difference, besides investing your own time and energy, is to convince other people that they should invest theirs. That's how you raise awareness and grow involvement so that you are able to do the most good and reach more children than ever before. I hope that everyone reading this book feels a little more motivated to get involved and a little more empowered in knowing that every person in every role who supports this great organization in some way is making a real and significant difference in the lives of seriously ill children by giving them the tremendous gifts of love, celebration, and hope. That's what matters. That's what we're all working toward.

RACING FOR SMILES

Jimmie Johnson

*I first learned about the importance of granting wishes
long before I ever became involved with Make-A-Wish. When
I was still a teenager racing in the Mickey Thompson stadium
series, all of the racers would get together for media days to travel
to a local children's hospital to visit with the patients.*

Sometimes, it was clear that the child and his or her family had been at the hospital for weeks or even months and was on a fast track to a full recovery. Some had been there for a long time as they ran out of treatment options; others were just arriving, and their futures were still unknown. But whatever the case, it was really moving to see how something as simple as a visit could put a smile on their faces. I knew that if I ever made it big, I wanted that kind of work to be one of my biggest priorities.

When I became affiliated with NASCAR, one of the first things I learned was the close association that NASCAR has with Make-A-Wish. They have the whole process down to a science in terms of navigating the pit passes and garage tours, and facilitating the families' visits. It was really awesome to see how well they were able to take care of all of the kids who wanted to come to the track. I thought, "That's exactly the kind of thing I want to be a part of!" I let Make-A-Wish know that I was already hooked on the whole wish-granting process, even though I'd never been part of an official one, and started helping Make-A-Wish with fundraisers and awareness campaigns. I even did a few commercials to help drum up support. Basically, I just wanted to be involved in whatever way they thought they could use me.

One of the first opportunities I had to participate with Make-A-Wish was through some of those extremely well-organized group visits that had impressed me in the first place. Several kids and their families were touring the racetrack and team facilities, and the drivers were invited to say hello if they wanted to. It didn't start out that anyone was specifically requesting to meet me, but I just couldn't turn down the opportunity to get involved. At one race in Michigan, when I was still pretty new to NASCAR, Make-A-Wish had set up a room with maybe forty kids and their families. It was a *huge* number of kids from around the state who wanted to attend a race and meet some of the drivers. To be honest, it was a little overwhelming to walk into a room that full, but a number of the drivers did it, and it was an absolute blast signing autographs and taking pictures. It was amazing that you could actually sit down and have a conversation with a family in the midst of all of that organized chaos, but somehow it happened and I was able to really connect with several of the kids there.

That experience, along with several others, made me decide that I would never, ever turn down the chance to grant a wish. And I haven't. My staff knows that if we get a request for a wish, it automatically goes on the schedule. They don't even need to run it by me to ask if it's something I want to do; they just find an available date and make it happen.

Sometimes, there are wish opportunities that aren't scheduled at all, but they are every bit as awesome. In November 2011, I met with a little guy who was at the track as part of his wish and was touring some of the "behind the scenes" areas. I

was on my way to my car because we had to get ready for our practice laps when he came zooming toward me in a golf cart, desperately wanting to say hi and talk to me. He had such an incredibly mature sense of humor that he had me absolutely rolling as we talked. It was one of the funniest conversations of my life, and we were both absolutely having a ball. Some people—kids and adults alike—just freeze when they meet you, but not this kid. He had so much charisma and wit; he'd say whatever was on his mind and just start talking with such intensity that it was impossible not to keep the conversation going. My crew was getting really anxious because time was ticking away, and when I finally said good-bye, I had to literally sprint to my car to make it in time, but I just couldn't bring myself to cut off our impromptu visit or cheat that kid out of any of my time that he wanted.

There was another meeting that we did that had an elaborate setup, where a

teenage girl who was a huge racing fan had just gotten well enough to earn her driver's license. She was so proud of herself and was so determined to be a good and safe driver (despite all the jokes about speeding like her favorite drivers on the track). It was arranged so that a policeman would pull her over and hidden cameras were rolling to film her reaction. The cop strode up to her car seriously, and the girl was absolutely panicking, trying to figure out what she'd done wrong and terrified that she was going to get a citation. She rolled down the window and the cop informed her, sternly, that she was going to Darlington Raceway and handed her tickets and passes for her whole family. It took her a second to realize what was really happening, and she could hardly believe it. She and her family came out and spent the weekend with my crew and me at the track. It was so much fun for everyone involved; sometimes those "experience"-type wishes, where there is a surprise situation and lots of volunteer involvement, can be the most gratifying not only for the child but for everyone involved in the planning and execution.

Despite the fun and laughter that wishes can bring to us all, it's important to remember the serious issues that these families are facing in their real lives. Not too long ago, just about a month after my daughter was born, I went to visit a children's hospital in Charlotte, North Carolina—the same one where my daughter had arrived into this world and brought such incredible joy to my family. But as I walked into the cancer ward and saw all of the critically ill children, the sadness, fear, and worry of other people's reality hit me. I met one family who showed me a short video from three weeks prior of their daughter running around perfectly healthy, chasing a ball in the backyard, laughing and yelling, just doing what a kid does—and there she was now, lying in the bed, hit with a sudden and extremely serious illness. She was on a ventilator and couldn't move, and the family simply had no clue what was going to happen. I left the hospital after that and had tears running down my face the entire drive home. Simply contrasting the fears and emotions with that family with my own

joy and excitement over my daughter's new life struck me deeply and reminded me of the importance of organizations like Make-A-Wish that provide support and encouragement not just to seriously ill children, but also to their families. Disease can happen to any one of us and turns our family's sense of normal upside down in a second.

Now, before every visit and every wish, I have to remind myself to stay positive, no matter what the situation. I make it my goal to not only keep smiling myself, but to make sure that everyone else involved is smiling, too. That's how I know that I've done my job—if, even for just the short time we spend together, the child and his or her family feel some happiness. I'll tease the kids or tell jokes or just talk quietly about whatever the kids are interested in until they come out of their shell. I just have to find a way to get them to start smiling. Once you get the smile, things start to roll. It's a great thing to grant a wish, but it's an even greater thing to know that the smiles have nothing to do with who you are or what you do on the track, but simply that you've lifted someone's spirits and are making their struggles a little easier.

THE BLESSING OF JOY

Bethany Hamilton

*When I was younger, I was always looking up to the older people
around me in my family, in my church, and in my community. Looking back, I
understand that it was so important for me to have role models as I grew up who
could help me make good decisions and not let the obstacles of life get me down.*

Especially after my accident, I found that positive influence so important as part of
the healing process, since my emotions sometimes felt as damaged as my body.
Knowing what an important role those mentors had held for me, I decided to try to do
the same thing for junior high school kids in my church youth group when I got to
high school—and I loved every challenging minute of it!

Knowing that I have been given a heart for being a positive influence on kids,
you can imagine how excited I was when Make-A-Wish contacted me about granting
wishes for seriously ill children. It was, and continues to be, such a great honor to get
to spend time with kids who are facing major health issues—and to get to encourage
them to keep fighting and keep approaching each day with an optimistic mind-set.
For me, it's a blessing to be a blessing.

Recently, I had the amazing experience of granting a wish for an eleven-year-old
girl named Cheyenne. She suffers from muscular dystrophy, which is an especially

big challenge for someone with so bright and active a mind as she has because her body can't keep up with her. We spent part of the day surfing and coordinated to be in the water at the same time with a group that takes people with various physical disabilities to the ocean to surf on specially designed boards for people in wheelchairs to make it safer or compensate for other physical challenges. They helped

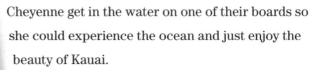

Cheyenne get in the water on one of their boards so she could experience the ocean and just enjoy the beauty of Kauai.

We also hung out at the swimming pool since she was able to move in the water with a completely different freedom than on dry land. As she swam, we talked nonstop the entire time. She had a million questions for me and was laughing and telling stories and jokes from the moment we got into the pool until the time we got out. I just assumed that she was naturally a bubbly, outgoing person because she seemed so at ease and comfortable, like she was best friends with everyone she'd ever met. But her mom told me later that Cheyenne had been facing some serious bullying at school because of her condition, which had made her worry that Cheyenne might have a difficult time coming out of her shell during her time with me during her wish. Clearly, though, that wasn't a problem.

"She hasn't talked that much in a year," her mom said with a big smile.

Wow.

That absolutely blew me away. I had no idea what Cheyenne was facing back home, and yet she felt she could rise above all of the hurt and sadness she'd experienced and be herself with me. I was tremendously humbled. I mean, what had I done to deserve her conversation? Who was I that she would feel she could show me her happiest, most real self? And yet, she had decided that she could trust me, and she gave me the wonderful gift of sharing her voice, thoughts, and personality. That was such an important reminder to me of the simple fact that we may not know what someone is going through, but a little bit of kindness can often help them power through it.

Last year I had another wish-granting experience that was incredibly moving. A seven-year-old girl named Kendall was undergoing treatment for leukemia and started watching my movie, *Soul Surfer*, in the process. She fell in love with the film, pulling out her dad's old surfboard and pretending to paddle out to catch waves in her front yard in Long Island, New York. She spent hours doing that and practicing "pop-ups" as if she had really caught a wave and was jumping to her feet to ride it in to shore. So when it came time for Kendall to ask for her wish, she knew exactly what she wanted: a chance to hang out with me and try surfing for real.

A major sports channel teamed up with Make-A-Wish as part of its wish-granting series and taped Kendall's wish experience, from the time she found out about it through our time together in Hawaii. I had such a great experience with the

entire family, surfing with Kendall and her sister and watching all that "lawn surfing" in the front yard paying off as Kendall caught several small waves and managed to ride them, standing up, all the way to shore. It was awesome! We've stayed in touch since her visit, and I've even been able to visit her in New York. I was just so impressed by her fearless attitude and precociousness, despite all of the aggressive treatments she's had to undergo to combat her cancer during her young life. It was so clear to me that Kendall and her entire family were positive people, and I like that we've become friends and that I've had a lasting influence on their lives. In fact, Kendall's mom will occasionally point to the fact that I am big on healthy eating in order to get her kids to make good food choices. She's told me things like, "Kendall just ate a salad because Bethany Hamilton eats salads!" I love that kind of thing so much because it reminds me of the fact that the impact of these wishes extends far beyond the day or two we spend hanging out. Sometimes I feel like I'm only able to offer temporary encouragement, but it is special being able to see how a real relationship can spring up between people that can help lift the spirits and shape the lives of everyone involved.

I have loved my time with every single wish child I have had the chance to meet. Sometimes, I will meet two or three kids at a time and grant those wishes together, and the kids seem to love getting to make new friends and hear answers to questions they might not have thought of themselves. I get asked everything from "What's your favorite color?" to "What is your favorite place to surf?" to "What was it like making the movie?" Sometimes, a child will even ask me, "Did it hurt when the shark bit you?" I've been asked that same question about a thousand times over the past ten years, so it doesn't faze me anymore. I just answer their questions honestly. I love that they are curious about all sorts of things and aren't afraid to speak up about whatever is on their minds. Usually, the kids want to try surfing, and some are even able to stand up on their boards, which is always really exciting for all of us. Other kids are okay with just paddling on the boards and floating, keeping things mellow as we just enjoy being in the water.

It's important to me to make sure that every child gets some quality one-on-one time, as well. We might spend a little more time in the water, talking about surfing or living in Hawaii or whatever else comes to mind, or we might do something as simple as coloring together—whatever they want to do. My family will sometimes have a barbecue back on the beach, and my mom will hang out with the families and show them how to make leis with local flowers. It's really a great time for everyone.

I try to make a point of not treating the children any differently than I would a healthy child. I think that is an important part of their Make-A-Wish experience. I know from personal experience how frustrating it can be when well-meaning people think that they have to treat you like you're fragile or incapable of doing things by yourself just because you've undergone a rough time physically. In my mind, these

kids have proven that they are *tougher* than most people because of the stuff they've endured. It is another reminder to me that I have been given a great opportunity because of my injury to reach people in a way that I never could have without it. I think the kids understand that even though our experiences are very different, I still can empathize with a lot of what they are going through: being scared, being confused, feeling sick and tired of hospitals and doctors and people seeming sad or upset around me, and wanting my life to be about more than one bad thing that happened to me.

After every wish, I am always overcome with feelings of gratefulness: I'm grateful that I've had the chance to meet such wonderful people, grateful for the opportunity to provide support to children going through difficult times, grateful that I can share God's love and be reminded of the importance of making the most of our time here on earth.

Every wish child I meet has something special about them that gets me fired up and excited to be a part of their healing journey. I am also struck by how uncertain life can be for seriously ill children, though, which is a lesson most people don't have to learn until much later in life. Most of the kids I have granted wishes for so far have

been younger ones—usually under fifteen—

and it always shakes me up a little bit when I realize that some

of them may not make it to adulthood, or even their teenage years. I have to fight back tears when those thoughts hit me, because the last thing I want to do is bring any kind of sadness to their special day. There was one little girl in Florida who reached out to me, but she passed away before we were able to meet in person. It was heartbreaking for me to lose her after I had known her just from a phone call; I can't even imagine what her family was experiencing, as they learned to face life without her. I pray for the sick children I meet, and for their families, as well. If all I can physically give them is a day or two of my time, or even just some long-distance communication, I hope that I can at least encourage them by letting them know that God loves them.

Life is supposed to be about giving back and sharing peace with the people around us through whatever means we've been given to do so. I am so happy that I get the chance to make that happen through Make-A-Wish. All of the visits and all of the children have shown me in a thousand ways how much joy we can all bring to one another's lives. Getting to spend time with brave young people like Cheyenne, Kendall, and all of the children I have met has meant more to me than I can ever really express. "My" Make-A-Wish kids remind me that everything happens for a reason and that we can never know how much strength we really have until we are faced with something bigger than ourselves . . . and that we can each be a ray of sunshine to someone else, no matter what we've gone through.

BUILDING RELATIONSHIPS
FOR THE ENTIRE FAMILY

Kurt Warner

*I was a new quarterback for the St. Louis Rams
when I found myself sharing lunch with a seriously ill boy
named Benjamin, and wondering why I was there.*

It wasn't that I didn't want to be there—I was absolutely thrilled to meet the young man—but I was completely confused as to why on earth, of all things he could have asked for, Benjamin wanted to meet *me*. "What? You've got to wish bigger than that," I kept thinking. "You get to choose one thing in the world, and it's to hang out with me at training camp?" That created a lot of pressure! I mean, what an awesome, amazing charge to make a day special as a sick child's one wish. What could I possibly do that would make this day worthy of his hopes? I was still new to the league. What could I give to him that would mean much more than a couple of hours with some guy who throws around a football for a living? I wanted to do something for him that was memorable and lasting. And that feeling grew as the day continued. The more time I spent with Benjamin and his family, the more I was humbled by their strength and resilience. I kept thinking to myself, "This is what courage looks like."

My day with Benjamin was before I launched my own foundation or started doing much philanthropy. It was the first time I was able to appreciate the position I

was in, as a sports figure, to give back in a special and unique way. People can ask you for an autograph, but to have someone at Make-A-Wish tell you a child's *one wish* is to meet you—it's overwhelming. That was the moment that made me realize what an impact I could have that went far beyond just a hug or a handshake or posing for a couple of pictures. That little boy opened my eyes to just how much encouragement someone in my position could provide. Up to that point, I don't think I had fully realized my own potential.

The more I thought about the tremendous bravery of that family, the more I came to understand that what I wanted to give to Benjamin and other children like him wasn't just an experience or a memory; I wanted to give them relationships. If I could give them more than just a onetime event—an actual connection, a lasting sense of caring, concern, friendship, and support—then maybe I could be getting closer to giving these kids something that was worthy of the trust they had put in me to offer up some cheer and encouragement. By establishing relationships, I wouldn't just be giving them a momentary wish, but a *lasting* wish. And I wanted to extend those relationships to the entire family so that parents and siblings could build on those friendships and networks and support groups, as well.

After all, a life-threatening illness doesn't just affect the patient; it affects everyone around them. Everyone in the family is dealing with different kinds of stresses and emotions, and they all need a web of encouragement to help them stay strong and deal with the exceptional challenges of their life. It's not just parents torn between spending time at the hospital and going to work to keep food on the table and insurance coverage, but also how one child's hospitalization can throw the lives of the other siblings into chaos as one child suddenly becomes the focus of everyone's attention and concern. The entire family dynamic changes; any plans for the future are put into a state of uncertainty. The parents need to know that they are not alone. They need to hear tips for making it through the toughest days, for juggling all of the new responsibilities and time demands, for coping with feelings of helplessness or guilt or frustration or whatever else might be plaguing them as they watch their sick child endure treatments and hospitalizations. Siblings need to know that they are not alone in the inevitable slew of emotions they are feeling, be it confusion, jealousy, anger, sadness, or any combination of them all.

So much has grown out of that one day with Benjamin more than ten years ago. Now, instead of just granting a wish or two at a time, every year we bring together up to ten children and their families to spend a week at a theme park, not only making memories as a family far away from hospitals and treatment centers but also forming support groups for the parents, siblings, and the children themselves. Of course, there is plenty of time in the parks with rides and shows and sightseeing, but we also spend time with the families so they can talk about their experiences and ask questions of other families who have been, or are right now, in a similar situation. We pray daily and include a praise-and-worship service; we try to stress the positive—that these children are miracles for hanging on and fighting as hard as they can, and that God is bigger than illness, bigger than stress, and bigger than pain. There are also opportunities for the parents to have time alone, almost like mini–date nights, so that they are able to reconnect and keep their marriage strong despite the fact that all of their attention is necessarily focused on their children right now. If anyone in the family is gloomy, it tends to be the parents because they see the big picture, but the kids always impress us with how to just attack life. We want to lift up the parents but make sure that the vivaciousness of all the children affected is celebrated, as well. That's why we also make sure the siblings of sick children receive as much of our attention as the wish kids do.

Time is scheduled for the parents to share their family's own story of diagnosis, treatment, emotional ups and downs, and maybe even recovery. It not only gives them a chance to talk about their unique, individual set of circumstances, but it also breaks down walls and opens so many doors for them to see how everyone in that room, in that group, really connects and how their stories are all intersecting. It lets them know, "I'm not the only one in the world who's dealing with this. I'm not the only one fighting these battles." If nothing else, it gives them a number they can call to connect with another family on days when it all seems a little too overwhelming. In many cases, we hear from parents afterward that the experience has helped make their children feel reenergized, far more hopeful, and far less alone after meeting other children like themselves. That's really what my wife and I wanted to accomplish when we decided to translate my experience with Benjamin into something larger. I wanted to do more than just sign a jersey or a football for a kid; I really wanted them to think, "Wow. I came here interested in Kurt Warner, but I left know-ing Kurt was interested in me." And I wanted the whole family to feel that way.

Brenda and I share with the families about our son Zack, who suffered a trau-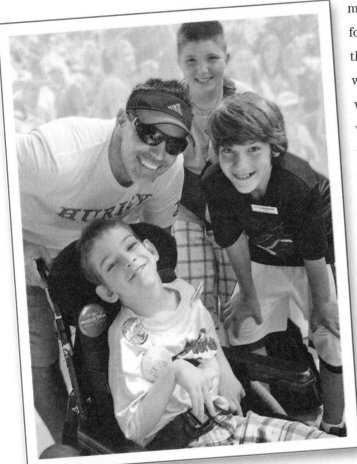matic brain injury when he was four months old. At the time, the doctors weren't sure if he would survive or, if he did, what his life would look like. It was a terrible time filled with worries and questions and fears about the future. But now, it's such a thrill to see Zack as a twenty-four-year-old, thriving and making the most of every day. While I know that my family's experience is not exactly the same as what the Make-A-Wish families are going through, I want to at least give them some hope that there is life on the other side of hospitals and treatments and rehabilitation and the like. But really, I try not to interject myself too much into the goings-on as the families connect. I want to make sure they under-stand that the time at the theme park is not about a week with Kurt Warner. It's about the relationships that come out of the time we all spend together; everything else is secondary. We get a chance to become real friends, and football just becomes something incidental.

My own children are involved, as well, forming friendships that last long after the week ends. They plan sleepovers and summertime visits and attend birthday parties of some of the friends they've made from our Make-A-Wish experiences.

When we first get together at the park, my kids recognize that there are going to be some limitations on what some of the children can do, but once they start talking and laughing together, it's as if that never crosses anyone's mind again and it's all about celebrating life together. It's been so great to get to move the families up to the front of lines and see them feel both incredibly special and incredibly normal at the same time as they connect with our kids and bond just like regular kids who don't have a care in the world. It's my family's favorite week of the year.

It's been such an incredible blessing for my own family to make these connections because I want them to understand that charity isn't about using money to give to someone else. It's about impacting someone—and the impact that has on you. It's about giving of yourself, your time, your emotional strength—whatever you have to give. I want them to leave exhausted from giving of themselves completely. I don't want my kids to miss that. I am always sad when it's time to leave, and my kids cry when we have to say good-bye to our new friends. It's incredible. What brings us together is something terrible—serious childhood illnesses are one of the most heart-wrenching things a family can experience—but what keeps us together are the bonds we form.

We have reunions every couple of years around the country with families in each area whom we've invited to the theme park week. Now that I have a little more time on my hands, we actually see many of the families a couple of times a year. I am always shocked when I get to see those kids who were so sick a year or two ago now strong and healthy and absolutely thriving. You see pictures and read e-mails about their recovery and what they are up to, but nothing can really prepare you for seeing them with your own eyes. A lot of times, it's hard to believe it's the same kid. What really makes my wife and me happy, though, is hearing how the families very often stay in touch on their own; the teenagers will get together and do things, or maybe the families that are local will come together in a group and go to one of my own kids' sports games or plays.

The families have touched us as much as we hope we've touched them, and as I first realized as I was sitting across from Benjamin, my very first wish child, looking in the faces of those children and their families really helps you understand what courage looks like—and that's been one of the greatest blessings of my life.

GIVING CHILDREN

A SENSE OF OWNERSHIP

Luis Gonzalez

When a child is diagnosed with a serious illness, his or her life

suddenly changes completely. Between doctors and nurses and

worried parents closely monitoring every symptom, change, or activity,

there isn't a whole lot that the kids themselves can control.

For a kid, it can be so important to get to feel a little bit of independence over their experiences or their life, and Make-A-Wish does just that by giving sick children a unique experience designed around their individual requests. It gives them something that they really need: ownership.

When I was growing up in Tampa, Florida, I was surrounded by positive examples of how role models can impact the lives of children. Probably the most important person who modeled this was my mother, a Cuban immigrant. She was a school teacher who instilled in me a deep love for helping kids and an appreciation for the many ways that children can be inspired simply because a responsible, caring adult took the time to reach out to them. As a kid, I remember what a thrill it was when the Cincinnati Reds came to town and the players for the Big Red Machine signed autographs and shook our hands during batting practice. I loved to try to get the attention of the Buccaneers players at football games. I couldn't think of a bigger thrill than to have those guys take a moment to sign something or talk to all of the children crowded along the railings. It just made me feel special. Sometimes, there would be players who would just ignore the kids, and I remember, very clearly, thinking to myself, "If I ever make it to the big leagues, I am not going to be that guy!"

Because of my mother's great work in the classroom (and support for my autograph chasing) and the encouragement that meeting those professional athletes gave me to chase my own dream, the first thing I did when I made it to the majors was to tell the team management, "I want to be involved with children's charities." First in Houston, then in Chicago, Phoenix, Los Angeles, Miami, and finally back in Phoenix again, I had the honor of working with kids in each city, helping special causes, and being involved in wishes. Over the years, my teammates and I spent a lot of time in hospitals, making visits and taking photos. I can't even describe the rush you experience when a kid hooked up to all kinds of tubes and machines breaks into a smile when you walk in the room. It's incredible. I always go back in my mind to when I was a little kid in the stands, so excited to meet one of my heroes; then I think about what it must be like for those kids who don't have the freedom to leave their treatment centers or even their beds to experience a game in person. How much more it must mean to them to know that their favorite players were thinking of them and that those fans motivate us just as much as the ones who are able to be there physically! Those hospital visits were an especially strong reminder for me to always make sure that I was never too busy to take the time to meet with children fighting life-threatening conditions.

Whenever the team's public relations office would contact the players to let us know that there would be a wish kid coming to the game with their family, I always made a special note to myself to keep an eye out for them. I wanted to make sure that, no matter what, I was able to get a chance to go over and say hi, maybe give a high five, sign an autograph, or toss them a ball. I wanted them to know that it was so special to me that they were there at the game. Sometimes they might be hooked up to machines that had to accompany them to the ballpark or they might have bruises or other marks on their bodies due to their treatment. Sometimes they simply looked tiny and frail. You don't want to let on how tough that is to see, of course, because you want to make sure that you stay smiling and happy for their special time. But after you say good-bye and take the field or go down into the dugout, you want to cry. I know that some guys struggle with meeting wish kids before the game because it can be so heartbreaking, and I completely understand that. But for me, whenever I knew a Make-A-Wish kid was in the crowd, that meeting was as essential as the pregame warm-up. Seeing someone who is going through so much find joy in watching me play gives me a profound sense of responsibility.

Whenever I grant a wish at a game for a kid who has specifically requested to meet me, I try to start it out immediately with a big hug to let the kid know that I am as excited about this as they are and to help break down any shyness they might have. What I really want the kid to get to see and feel is the sense of the routine that exists for a major league ball club before a game. Most kids seem to find that a neat behind-the-scenes glimpse that they haven't ever seen on TV, and I think it makes them feel like they have special "insider's knowledge" that they can carry with them after our visit is over. When I take them around to meet the other twenty-four players, the manager, and the various coaches, I always try to frame it as, "Let me introduce you to my friends!" Sometimes, I think the experience can be a little overwhelming at first to be in that stadium they've seen on TV so many times, or to be surrounded by the players they've watched but maybe never considered were "real people." I love the openness and honesty of the kids. They all seem to have an authenticity about them, as if going through everything they've had to go through has made them realize that while good manners matter, life is too precious to not just cut to the heart of things.

Once, when I was granting a wish for one boy in Arizona, I asked him why he had chosen to meet me for his wish. "Well, actually, you were my second choice," he said. "The singer I had originally asked to meet couldn't do it, so then I wished for you." That made me laugh so hard!

And I always try to make sure that my wish kids get a specific part of their wish that belongs to them alone. Whether it's getting to go into the locker room to meet the starting pitcher fifteen minutes before the game or playing catch on the field, I'll tell the parents, "He's with me—don't worry about him." As I said earlier, for kids whose every move is (necessarily) monitored by parents and medical staff alike, getting complete ownership of a moment that no one else can claim can be a big deal. I don't mean any disrespect toward the families, of course. But I think it's really meaningful for the kids who are sick and have basically lost any kind of control over their lives to get to experience something that makes their parents say, "Wow! I wish I could have done that." But the kids can say, "Nope. That was just me. I got to do that myself."

After every wish or meeting with a wish child, I always go home and tell my wife about who I got to meet that day, and then I hug my own kids—triplets Megan, Jacob, and Alyssa—extra tight. Seeing the heartache that some families must go through always makes you more aware of the blessings in your own life that you don't always stop to think about as often as maybe you should.

About ten years ago, I got the chance to grant a wish for an eleven-year-old boy named Tyler, who had brain cancer. It was one of our first games of the season, in April, and Tyler had just finished his last chemo treatment in March, so the wish came almost like a celebration for having beaten his cancer. He got picked up from school in a white stretch limo that whisked him and his family to our stadium. They started out with dinner at the restaurant in our stadium and then went to watch batting practice and the game. Tyler was very excited to have been dubbed an honorary batboy. I was very excited that he was wearing my number on his T-shirt.

"It's my lucky shirt," he explained, and I was absolutely thrilled.

We went down into the dugout and toured the clubhouse where he was able to meet my teammates and get a bunch of autographs on his batting helmet. My goal was to make Tyler feel like he was part of the team. But then, something happened that made that night unforgettable. Just before he had to go to his seat and I had to line up for the game to start, I rubbed his lucky shirt. There must have been some-

thing to it, because I hit a home run early in the first inning of the game. I tried to find him in the crowd as I was running the bases, because I needed to point to him to thank him for helping that big moment happen. There is a swimming pool in our stadium, just beyond the right field wall, and that's where Tyler was watching the game with family and friends. The ball sailed right by them as they cheered. It just seemed a little surreal. You obviously want to make sure that you do something special in the games when you have a kid there who is cheering for you, but it doesn't always happen. I felt like that day, though, it was one of those things that was just meant to be.

Even though I am retired from playing baseball now (which means there probably won't be any more kids specifically requesting to meet me), I still try to stay active with Make-A-Wish to show them my support in whatever way I can, and I still work with the Diamondbacks in our outreach and efforts to support groups dedicated to making a difference in the lives of kids. I love that the owners and managers are dedicated to going above and beyond just talent when looking for players. They genuinely have a concern for those athletes who will give back to the community. One of the reasons I am so proud to be a part of the Diamondbacks family is their organization-wide emphasis on helping foundations like Make-A-Wish.

In 2012, the team donated $50,000 to the Summer of Wishes program, which sought to help fund wishes for the kids in Arizona still waiting for their wish to be granted. Did you know that the average amount of time between when a child makes a wish and is able to have it granted is close to nineteen months? It's not only that there are the challenges with coordinating the wish around treatment plans and checkup schedules, but there is also the simple issue of fund-raising. It is not cheap or easy to bring a wish to reality, so as a result, much of the wait time is often tied to being able to find the money to make it happen. And when kids are diagnosed with particularly aggressive conditions, it can be a race against the clock to give them a chance to create these special memories from their wish.

In 2009, I had the opportunity to serve as the honorary chairman of the Make-A-Wish golf tournament for the Arizona chapter, and I absolutely jumped at the chance. It was hosted by a golf club in Chandler, Arizona, and so many different people came out to support the kids. Besides the golf tournament itself and the silent auction, a military helicopter from one of the local bases was there for the families to look inside, and there were all sorts of activities and events for the kids. I was eager to be a part of their work to raise funds to help make more wishes come true and to bring them about more quickly. It is a cause that is important to my entire family.

My parents lived the American dream, and their hard work gave me a chance to chase my own future. I got to put on a big-league uniform and play a kids' game for nearly twenty years. I got to live my dream, too. But those kids battling serious illnesses? That's nothing they asked for, nothing they hoped about. I want to help give them the greatest gift of all—the dream of just being a normal kid with a life that is their own. If my career can put a smile on a child's face simply because they watched me run around a field chasing a ball, then I feel like I have an obligation to use that platform to do the most possible good. It's the least I can do. If spending a couple of hours with me ahead of a game gave them a break from their time in hospitals and instead give them a sense of ownership over just one little portion of their lives, even if everything else is out of their control, I can't think of anything more important or more meaningful.

Tyler, the child with brain cancer, is now in his twenties and planning to become an RN; his time spent in hospitals as a child had a major impact on his career decision and gave him tremendous empathy for other people. As his mother, Christine, recalls, "There were two treatment options for Tyler. One was the traditional treatment, but the other was an experimental one. Immediately, Tyler said he wanted to be part of the experimental treatment. He said, 'If it helps one little kid not have to go through what I'm going through, it's worth it.'" Christine believes that Make-A-Wish provides an important part of the treatment and healing process for the children it serves.

"It's always good to have Mom and Dad there when you go through everything," she said. "But Mom and Dad can't make it all go away for a while. They can't take away worry about when the next shot or injection is due. But with the wish, it's a whole day where nothing goes wrong."

THE EXPERIENCE
WILL CHANGE YOU

Grant Hill

My first introduction to Make-A-Wish was roughly twenty years ago, when I was still in college. I remember driving over from Durham to the hospital in Chapel Hill and sitting down with a boy in his hospital room. He had a terminal brain tumor, but he was a sweet kid and so happy to have a special visitor.

I couldn't believe that a child so young could be shouldering a load so heavy, but as we sat and talked, I not only learned more about that child but also got to witness his incredible spirit. I was so inspired and so humbled—and I knew that I was hooked on wish granting. It seemed like such a tremendous honor to be asked to be a part of making a child's wish come true. It wasn't an ego thing; it was more a sense of a profound responsibility to make sure I was reaching out to impact someone who really deserved my attention.

Since then, I have been fortunate enough to be invited to meet dozens of wish kids, either at their homes or in hospital rooms or at games or in our practice facility, and I have been affected and touched by every single experience. Often, as a professional athlete, it's easy to get lost in your own little universe. You get so caught up in your own individual performance and your team's record that the ups and downs of a season become a roller coaster of emotions that can consume you. (And as Tamia, my wife, likes to say, if it affects you, it affects the whole family!) You're removed from some of the real-life troubles in the world as you live in a bubble, and you can sometimes lose sight of the fact that what you do, ultimately, is just play a game. But when you have the chance to sit down with a seriously or terminally ill child, that bubble bursts and you are able to view reality again with true perspective.

I'm always amazed by how much I take from each and every meeting with a wish child. It's not only the wonderful example they all provide of positive thinking and tremendous courage but also the sense of awe that one person really can make a difference in someone else's life. When that child looks at you and says—whether out loud or just with their eyes—"I am fighting to survive. I could have anything at all, and I picked *you* to make me feel better for a day," you cannot *not* be changed by that. So you immerse yourself in the moment and have as much fun as possible interacting with the child for that day and trying to make them smile, laugh, and create happy memories. But later that night, after you've gone home and had a chance to really digest the day, you cannot help but wonder, "Why are there so many things I'm worried about that don't really matter?" That's one of the things that I believe makes the wish process so special: it not only gives the child hope, but also helps to revive and recenter the wish granters.

I always talk to my wife and children afterward, telling them about the child I met and reviewing with my own family how very much we have to be thankful for. We've had our own challenges, of course—I've had some injuries that have limited my playing time, and Tamia was diagnosed with multiple sclerosis about ten years ago—but nothing we've faced compares to what these families have had to contend with. Overall, we are healthy and tremendously blessed. Sometimes, you just need a reminder that, at the end of the day, there are only a handful of things that are really important: family, close relationships, health, and a sense of peace. Much beyond that is just icing on the cake. So when you meet a family whose world has been rocked by a life-changing diagnosis, it usually makes whatever worries were rattling around in your own mind seem a whole lot pettier.

I think it makes you reconsider the importance of your own contributions to the lives of others as well when you witness something as simple as a pair of basketball shoes or an autographed card lift someone's spirits so much. I have something of a unique perspective on the impact of meeting a childhood icon, because I was lucky enough to have a father who was also a professional athlete and who took me along to meet some of his peers. I will never forget meeting guys like Franco Harris and Tony Dorsett, who played with my dad in the NFL. I also got to meet pro basketball players like Patrick Ewing and Julius Erving (or, as he's better known, "Dr. J"). Even now, decades later, I can still remember exactly where I was when I got to meet Dr. J. Whenever I see him on TV or read an article about him, I'm immediately a ten-year-old kid again, and all of the excitement and wonder come rushing back to me. I remember the anticipation I felt ahead of meeting him and how I was determined to be on my best behavior on the days before so I wouldn't miss out, and the thrill of imagining the stories I would be able to tell my friends afterward. I was so motivated by the chance to meet someone I looked up to so much that it drove everything I did leading up to that day.

While it's certainly not exactly the same, I think that experience is very similar to a major component in the Make-A-Wish process. When a child has something to look forward to, something to aim for, it helps to make some of the more unpleasant things more bearable. If a child knows that enduring the pain of injections or the illness brought on by chemotherapy or the fatigue of rehab will make him or her able to enjoy that special day more thoroughly, then maybe the treatment doesn't seem quite so bad. I think it even serves the child's family in a similar way, too. Mom, Dad, siblings—they've all had to be so strong to support not only the sick child but each other, as well. If they know that a good day is coming that will be about something other than the illness or treatment, it gives them a reprieve. So if the buildup to a wish can give everyone in the family a little more motivation and strength to keep powering through, then you can't place a value on that.

Whenever I grant a wish, I try to make sure that everyone in the family feels uplifted, but I also want to make sure that the wish child is my main focus. It's always interesting to me that the thing the kids seem to enjoy the most isn't necessarily the most exciting part of the day—that is, watching the practice or the game. What they seem to like best is the one-on-one time when we sit down and just hang out like friends. The kids ask all kinds of questions, so you never know what to be prepared for. Some might want to know what it is like playing in the NBA or who my inspirations are. Others may start out asking about my favorite food. Some come in with a list of questions they've been working on for months that cover everything they've ever wanted to know about me. Some kids are terribly (and adorably) shy and just freeze up when I say hello. In those cases, I try to stress that the day is all about them, not me. If they think of questions they want to ask me, that's great, but I'm there to get to know them—the day is about what they like to do and whatever they want to talk about. No matter what the child's personality, it's always something of a ride, and I love it.

I have to admit, though: there is certainly a learning curve on the part of wish granters. When I was in college and just starting out in the pros, I probably wasn't as good at making the experience memorable for the child as I would have liked to have been. I think back to that very first visit I made and to several subsequent ones, and I know I was a little awkward and probably kind of clumsy as I attempted to bond with the child. I was an only child, and both my parents were only children, so I didn't grow up with younger siblings or cousins around. Aside from my friends at school, I didn't really have much experience with other kids. So my life experiences were still fairly limited back in college, and I felt overwhelmed by the magnitude of what these families were facing. I also didn't have kids of my own, so I wasn't as comfortable with how to interact with children. Confidence and maturity played into things, too, I'm sure; after all, for those first few wishes, I was still practically a kid myself. Now that I am a parent, though, I think that I'm not only better able to connect with kids, but also better able to understand what the parents are experiencing. From the moment you first see your child in the delivery room, you are filled with love like you have never known before . . . as well as worry, concern, and fear. Parenting is the most fulfilling thing you will ever do, but also the most nerve-wracking. You will second-guess yourself constantly. You will stay up at night fretting about if you handled something the wrong way or thinking about what will become of your child. Even though I have been fortunate enough to never deal with a serious illness with either of my daughters, I think that simply becoming a parent has allowed me to empathize a little better by understanding just a tiny fraction of what stresses and hurt the families must be feeling. But when I try to multiply that by what the parents must be going through when they see all that their child is facing and they know that they are, essentially, powerless? It blows me away.

Parenthood has changed me as a wish granter, but as with anything, I think practice makes perfect. Each wish I granted was a little better, a little smoother, and seemed a little more natural. But it never becomes easy; I don't think anything like this ever could be. I don't always know the ins and outs of what these children are going through, but I do know that if they qualify for a wish, then it's something pretty serious. That's impossible to get out of your head. I am fortunate enough to have had the chance to meet so many of these brave kids; from Duke to Detroit to Orlando, as my career advanced, I met more and more children who taught me how to be a better wish granter for the next child. By the time I got to Phoenix, I was far more prepared than I had been ten years before. That's a good thing, because the Arizona chapter of Make-A-Wish was incredible, organizing a number of visits for children to come to our practice facility to watch us work and then to meet with the entire team afterward. Sometimes, the kids might sit in with us for a film session as we watched the other team's game reels, or they might put on a jersey and join us in the huddle. Even though being present for a practice may not be quite as intense as attending a game, it meant that our time with the wish kid wasn't rushed either by the start clock or by the fact that we were fatigued after competing.

Those team visits were an absolute blast for all of us and seemed to help bring all the players together, almost like a team-building exercise, as we tried to make the day as special as possible for the children there. I loved the give-and-take with NBA player Steve Nash, who is absolutely incredible with wish kids. I especially enjoyed getting to grant wishes alongside him. It was kind of amazing to see the impact that meeting those children had on us as a group, because it helped remind us of what we represent as a team and why we do what we do—entertain, energize, and inspire—and how fortunate we are to have what we do. It's about so much more than the fame or the money, but when you're surrounded by that kind of celebrity, it's too easy to lose your focus.

When we grant wishes, however, we are able to see the kind of positive impact we can have on someone's life and how amazing that really is. I think that speaks volumes for the kind of people you have on your team when everyone is so invested in making wishes come true together in such a special way. Now that I am with the Los Angeles Clippers, I hope that I will have the opportunity to meet with wish children in Southern California and learn from them, as well. Those wishes may be a big deal for the kids, but I can promise you that they are a big deal for me, as well.

I wish that there were no need for Make-A-Wish. I wish that there would never be another child with a serious diagnosis. But that's not the world that we live in. I think about my own little girls and imagine what life would be like for them, and for Tamia and me, if either of them were facing a life-threatening illness or battling a gravely serious condition. I honestly can't imagine anything more challenging or upsetting, nor can I imagine how happy I would feel if I knew that other people cared enough to take the time to let my child know that she matters and that her courage matters. And I'll keep granting wishes as long as there is a child who wants to meet me, and I know Make-A-Wish will keep supporting families and children for as long as there is a need.

PAYING IT FORWARD

Chris Petersen

When a nurse first suggested referring twelve-year-old Stephen to Make-A-Wish, his parents were reluctant. "We didn't want our experience to take away from other children getting a wish," his mother, Betsy, explained. "But the nurse told us that that wasn't how it worked—they work to grant wishes for any child who qualifies."

Stephen then spent several weeks dreaming up possibilities: cooking with a celebrity chef, taking an Alaskan cruise, or serving in the military for one day. But finally, he hit upon the perfect idea: "My favorite wish would be to coach for Boise State."

"Do you mean you want to play for Boise State?" his parents asked. He had wanted to play football before his cancer diagnosis and had recently been honored at a local high school football game.

"No," Stephen assured them. "I want to coach."

Boise State had, after all, been his favorite team ever since he was five years old. He just happened to once see a game on TV and was completely and utterly hooked. Stephen's family is from Texas, has no connection to Boise, and had never been to Idaho, but something about the Broncos captured Stephen's heart, and they were his team from then on out. So when some representatives from Make-A-Wish showed up to meet with Stephen and ask him about his wish, his mother was shocked when Stephen blurted out, "I want to do a shopping spree."

As soon as the representatives packed up and left, Stephen broke down crying. When his mother asked him what was the matter, he told her he had really wanted to ask to be a coach but had been afraid to because he had been dealt so many disappointments with his health that he didn't want to face another one since he knew that his wish was a long shot.

Betsy immediately called Make-A-Wish and explained the situation, and they said they would work on it. They said they weren't sure if they could get him on the field as a coach, but they were sure they could get him to a game, though he might have to wait a year since it was the end of September and the season was already in full swing. Stephen said that would be okay and he would wait as long as it took.

"Less than two weeks later," Betsy recalled, "I got a call saying that everything was arranged and Stephen could coach." The request had reached the Idaho chapter of Make-A-Wish just as some of the staff were having lunch with Barbara Petersen, my wife. They read the request to her, and she said, "Let me call my husband."

I immediately agreed and assured them I would make it happen. And just like that, the pieces all started to come together for Stephen to join the coaches for the November 6 game against the University of Hawaii Warriors.

I am the head coach of the Boise State Broncos. I am part of one of the most dynamic programs in all of college football. But before all of that, I am a dad. And that's where my story with Make-A-Wish begins. When my youngest son, Sam, was thirteen months old, he was diagnosed with a brain tumor. Despite undergoing treatment, by the time he was two and a half, the cancer had spread to his spine. Eventually, even though the cancer seemed to be responding, his medical team recommended that we consider radiation treatment to completely eradicate whatever cells were left. They warned us, however, that such intense treatment on so young a child would likely have lasting effects on his physical and mental development, and he would probably never be able to live independently as an adult. The decision was ours.

It was a heartbreaking, gut-wrenching time as we discussed every possibility, every pro and con of either undergoing or waiving the radiation. Finally, we decided to just progress with the treatment track we were on and bypass the radiation. More than a decade later, after chemotherapy, a stem cell transplant, and more chemo, we have a healthy, happy, active fourteen-year-old the doctors have nicknamed the "Miracle Kid." But the road to where we are now was long and exhausting.

What many people do not realize is that when a child goes into the hospital for a serious illness, the entire family goes into the hospital. Parents, siblings—they all end up sleeping on chairs or cots or even on the floor. The diagnosis may be for just the patient, but it affects everyone's life. Together with my wife and our oldest son, Jack, we basically camped out in Sam's hospital room during some of his treatments. Any family going through something like that understands that a sense of together-ness is far more important than physical comfort.

When Sam was eight, one of his medical caregivers referred him for a wish; we don't know who it was who submitted his name, but we will always be grateful. Once Make-A-Wish reviewed Sam's file and contacted us to inform us that he was eligible to ask for a wish, we weren't sure at first what to think. I had taken over at Boise State by then and felt it might not be fair for us to get a wish when there were other families who might have bigger needs. But what I learned impressed me so much; what I did professionally didn't matter because the wish wasn't about me. It was all about giving Sam a special time away from his treatments and granting him a wonderful experience that would be all his.

Sam thought about it for a long time, talking about various possibilities and trying to settle on exactly the right one. From a parent's perspective, it was the greatest thing in the world to see my son so focused on something that took his mind away from his illness. He felt so unbelievably proud that he would get to call the shots on his own special day, and finally settled on a trip to San Diego for the whole family. We visited an exciting aquatic theme park, which was great for the whole family, and then spent a day at a family fun park that he'd always wanted to visit, where he was shown how the toys they had there were built, and then got to spend over an hour building an action figure. As I watched my boys' faces light up, I knew that this experience was far more meaningful than any normal trip we could have taken together just as a family.

As for Sam, I can't even begin to describe how important that wish was for him. It gave him so much energy, enthusiasm, and excitement to anticipate a day that was just for him and, in some ways, got to be almost like his gift to the family. Make-A-Wish absolutely won my heart during that experience.

Fast-forward a few years to November 2010, when I was contacted by Make-A-Wish about a boy named Stephen Kinsey from San Antonio, Texas, whose wish was to be a coach for the Broncos. Honestly, my first thought was "Does he have the wrong Broncos? He must mean the Denver Broncos, not the Boise State Broncos." But he was a fan, and his wish was to be coach for a day—and the question was, would I be willing to host him and his family?

It was one of the most exciting moments of my life. I could not believe that I was in a position to make some other child's wish come true, after being so grateful for the wonderful experience my own child had with his wish. I couldn't agree fast enough.

But as soon as I did, I suddenly panicked. What on earth can I do to make this day live up to his hopes and *my* hopes of the experience I'd like to give him? That

was when I learned just how many people it takes to pull off a fantastic wish, as well as how many folks are eager to get involved when they learn about the child's visit.

Just over a month after making his request, Stephen, his parents, and his two younger siblings were en route to the game, waiting to board their plane after a layover in Phoenix, when the gate agent made an announcement that Stephen was on his way to receive his wish to coach the Broncos; all of the passengers burst into applause. Once they boarded the plane, a flight attendant approached the family and said some passengers were curious if this was the boy they'd been reading about in all the Boise papers. Betsy was amazed that they would have recognized her son's story and remembered his name. She had no idea how excited Boise was to welcome their newest coach or about the plans they had in place to roll out the red carpet for his arrival.

When the family arrived at the Boise airport, my wife, sons, several members of the Make-A-Wish board of Idaho, and a number of people from the community were there to greet them. "There was a huge crowd waiting to welcome us at the airport," Betsy said. "There were electronic road signs on the highway that read, 'Welcome to Boise, Coach Kinsey.' People were sending food over to our table at restaurants and dropping off gifts at the hotel. Our wonderful hotel even agreed to ship home for us four huge boxes of souvenirs people had delivered for us. We were on TV and in the newspapers—it was like we were celebrities! . . . It seemed like everyone in Boise who brought us gifts brought something for all of our children so that it wasn't just about Stephen, but about his siblings, Bethany and Jonathan, too."

When they got to their hotel, they found that their room had been decked out in Broncos colors and paraphernalia by the hotel's owner. It was wonderful to see how many people were willing to go the extra mile to make the Kinseys feel welcome and special. When Stephen came to campus, he got a tour of the facilities including the locker room, hall of fame, and our training gym. We spent some time in my office as well as at practice, and he was able to join some of our players for lunch.

On game day, we had a special surprise in store for "Coach Kinsey." We have a tradition at Boise State home games that one player who has distinguished himself that week gets to carry a sledgehammer, symbolizing hard work and drive, as he runs out at the front of the team onto our famous blue turf. Our players—who all called Stephen "Coach" while he was there—met together beforehand and agreed that they wanted Stephen to carry out the sledgehammer alongside the player of the week, but they wanted to make sure that he was able to carry it and could be out front. So they found him a smaller sledgehammer and agreed to walk rather than run behind him, to show their support.

It was such a powerful moment when the music was blaring, the crowd was going wild, the fog machines were creating drama—and out came Shea McClellin, our sledgehammer man of the week, holding hands with Stephen, with the rest of the team following them. I was the last one out of the tunnel, and I could hear the crowd absolutely erupting louder than I had ever heard them before. They weren't just shouting for us—they were cheering and clapping for Stephen, who then joined the rest of the coaches on the sidelines and helped lead the team to victory. It was just a great, great day.

For me, one of the most impactful parts of it was not only realizing the unique privilege I had to interact with the Kinsey family and make their time with us special, but also seeing how quickly and enthusiastically our students rallied around Stephen. College students often don't have enough experience to really grasp the full picture of what a family of a seriously ill child is experiencing. Our student athletes are about as healthy as people can possibly be, so I have to admit that I wondered if they would be able to empathize with the Kinseys. But as soon as our players met the Kinseys, everyone seemed to rally together and interact with Stephen in a way that showed me all those fears were unfounded. We had such a great connection, in fact, that the Kinseys have stayed in touch with our team and are proud members of the Boise State family!

The following year, we had the opportunity to grant a wish for an eight-year-old boy from Georgia. He helped out in practice, met all the cheerleaders and our mascot, Buster Bronco, was part of the pregame coin toss, and coached on the sidelines during the game. He was such an amazing kid and so much fun to hang out with. It was an honor to have him be a part of our team.

We've recently learned that we have another wish coming up for a child from Minnesota. I am so excited to get to host another wish child and family and to make their big day every bit as special.

In some ways, it seems like the experience of a serious illness can be harder on the parent than on the sick child because we understand the gravity of the situation and are aware of what complications could arise during the course of treatment and of the lasting results of either the illness, treatment, or both. Especially when the child is younger, he or she is usually not aware of all of the possible outcomes. It is terribly difficult to look at your child and feel powerless. Having an organization like Make-A-Wish step in and say, "We're looking out for you, and we want you to know you're not alone" lifts such a heavy burden off our shoulders. Even though they can't take away the pain or discomfort our child is feeling, and even if they can't provide a cure-all for the situation, they give our child happiness and hope in the anticipation of the wish, the experience of it, and in the memories it creates.

After the Kinseys returned home, Betsy admitted she was afraid that it might seem like kind of a letdown after the incredible whirlwind of Boise.

"But people still call for interviews sometimes. The papers up there still carry stories about Stephen," she said. "People send him birthday cards, and the team even made him a birthday video last year. Mrs. Angela Harvey's fifth-grade class at Les Bois Junior High has celebrated 'Coach Kinsey Day' for the past two years. She tells them about Stephen, and they learn about childhood cancer and then make him get-well cards. The people of Boise are just amazing. They have become dear, dear friends to us."

The year after Stephen's big day, the Kinseys were invited back to be a part of the Serving Up Wishes gala for the Idaho chapter of Make-A-Wish, which allowed them to renew and strengthen some of those friendships. Betsy laughed: "I would walk to the moon and back for Make-A-Wish after what they did for our family."

Stephen's treatments continue, as do the Kinseys' challenges as a family. Bethany, who is now twelve, had to have a pacemaker installed when she was three years old and was recently diagnosed with type 1 diabetes. Jonathan, seven, has been battling an immune deficiency disorder since infancy. "We are very used to doctors and hospitals," Betsy explained. "But other than our three children and their diagnoses, nothing has changed our lives so much as our time in Boise."

In May of 2013, Stephen, now fourteen, had to undergo a bone marrow transplant to treat his cancer. His doctor asked him if he had three wishes, what they would be. Stephen replied, "One, I wish I didn't have to have a transplant. Two, I wish my counts were good every time I get tested. Three, I wish I didn't feel bad all the time."

Betsy looked at her son and asked him, "Why didn't you wish you didn't have cancer in the first place?"

Stephen answered simply, "Because if I didn't have cancer, I wouldn't have Boise."

ATTITUDE IS EVERYTHING

Annika Sorenstam

People always talk about how teenagers have "attitude problems."
Well, in January 2008, I met a fourteen-year-old full of attitude—and it was
exactly the kind of attitude I wish more people brought to their own lives.

I should explain, first of all, how it is that I got to meet that amazing girl with her amazing attitude. You see, initially, I didn't think I would ever have anything to offer Make-A-Wish. When you first start making a name for yourself on the professional scene, there are a lot of organizations that approach you, and you start hearing a lot of different names. I had known of Make-A-Wish for quite a while, but I didn't really think they'd ever call on me for anything. I knew they did fantastic work, but I didn't ever consider that I might end up involved with them, because I didn't really think anyone would be interested in meeting me. I'm a golfer—not many kids find that as exciting as, say, going to a theme park.

But that all changed in a rather surprising way in 2008. I was hosting a sponsor summit with all of my sponsors in one room as we discussed the direction of my career and my brand. I had ideas for my own foundation that I wanted to establish, but I also wanted to work with other nonprofits whose mission I supported and whose work I respected. I'd finally had a chance to meet with some of the organizers and staff of Make-A-Wish and knew I wanted them to be part of the conversation, because after hearing just a few stories, I was hooked.

So we invited Make-A-Wish to the summit to discuss possible ways that I could pitch in and help add some visibility to the organization—nothing specific, just whatever they needed me to do to help endorse their goals. But as luck would have it, I got the chance to do something a lot more focused than just lending them my name. As we were all sitting together talking about different options for work I could do, an e-mail came through for one of the Make-A-Wish representatives. She looked down at her phone and then said, "You won't believe it, but . . ." And then she read us the message stating that there was a seriously ill child whose wish was . . . "*to play a round of golf with the world's greatest golfer—male or female—Annika Sorenstam.*"

It was kind of amazing, but I was every bit as surprised by the request itself as I was with the timing. It didn't make sense to me that a child could ask for anything he or she could imagine, and the child wanted to spend time with *me*. Why would any kid want to be in my shoes? But when a request like that is handed to you, you don't consider whether you say yes or no; you just want to see what you need to do to make it happen.

Once I had a chance to meet Molly, however, I immediately understood what a unique girl she really was. As a freshman in high school, Molly was a promising member of her high school's golf team. But when she was diagnosed with Hodgkin's lymphoma, a cancer of the lymph nodes, she had to put her game aside to focus on treatment. She had such a positive attitude, though, that all she really wanted to do was get back out on the links and keep growing as an athlete. So when she was approached by Make-A-Wish, she knew exactly what she wanted to ask for: a chance to play a round with—and ask for pointers from—another female golfer.

I have to admit that I was a little nervous about meeting her at first. I didn't know the right way to handle the issue of her illness. Did I ask her about it and show concern for her health? Or did I ignore it, striving to give her a day without having to think about it? Would it be rude to talk about it or would it be awkward not to, like the eight-hundred-pound gorilla in the room?

Admittedly, the day started out a little bit shyly, with our conversation consisting mostly of, "Hi, how are you?" "I am fine. How are you?" But before long, we were cracking jokes, laughing in the lunchroom, and giving each other hugs. Her parents and three siblings joined us, and together they spoke about the cancer, but in a detached way—like it was part of their reality but not something that consumed their lives. It was as if they refused to give it any more power or influence in their lives than it had already stolen. It was, I have to say, inspiring—almost as if they were there to do something for *me*.

Molly herself was very mature for a fourteen-year-old. I think she had been around so many adult conversations and had to interact with so many doctors and nurses that she couldn't help but reflect that influence, not to mention the fact that she had been dealing with some really grown-up stuff. But her tremendous enthusiasm for golf was what impressed me the most. Right away, I fell in love with her spirit and determination. Instead of asking for something that would give her a break from the hard work of recovery, Molly wanted to look ahead to her life postcancer. Not beating the disease was simply not an option for her; cancer was only an obstacle that would ultimately make her stronger in the pursuit of her dream.

We played nine holes at my ANNIKA Academy, a program I run to promote golf and fitness for children and teens, so the venue was perfect for a young lady who wanted to work on her game. My sponsors were really outstanding in making the day special, too, furnishing Molly with new golf clubs, golf clothes, and sunglasses, and providing her family with a gift basket during their three-day stay at the resort. Molly looked like a real professional, and I had so much fun talking to her about her

swing and grip as we played. We got to do some coaching as well as just hitting the ball. She asked me questions about what it's like "being a girl and being a pro," but she didn't stop there. She wanted to know what my day-to-day life was like. What was it like to travel all over the world? Did I know a lot of other famous golfers? What did we talk about? She wanted to hear about what it's like in college and how that is different from professional sports. She was so excited to learn everything she could about the world of golf beyond her high school team. Her hometown was pretty small, and most of the time she played against boys. I told her about how my sister and I were often the only two girls competing when we grew up, so we had to play against the boys, too.

The whole day, I was continually impressed by how strong Molly's mind-set was—that losing this fight against cancer simply was not an option. She was more than optimistic about the future—she was downright positive that it was going to be everything she had hoped and worked for. It was just amazing to see a teenager with so much determination and resolve. I absolutely loved my time with Molly and her family, and felt the tremendous honor of being asked to be a part of her special wish. What I didn't know was that three years later, I would be drawing upon that experience to help my family through its own huge challenge.

On March 21, 2011, my son Will was born at twenty-seven weeks by emergency C-section because of a detached placenta. He was only fifteen inches long and weighed 2.12 pounds. With any baby that premature, there was a laundry list of possible health problems. His lungs were one of the main concerns, but the doctors were quickly able to get him breathing, which was a huge blessing. However, he had to remain in neonatal intensive care for fifty-seven days. It was absolutely excruciating to have to see him in the incubator, fighting for his life. On the selfish side, we were so sad not being able to bring him home to be with our daughter, Ava, and not getting to hold him whenever we wanted.

But even as we were struggling through that difficult time, I kept thinking about Molly and her family. It was a comfort to know that we were not alone in our experiences. Of course, you don't want anyone else to have to go through the pain of having a seriously ill child; but when you can look to others and see that they pulled together and made it through, it gives you a reason to keep hoping and the strength to get out of bed in the morning. Our situations were very different, of course, but I realized that the need for a strong, positive attitude was still the same. You have to believe that you are going to beat the challenge or else you will struggle to find the strength to even function. Your attitude absolutely has to be one of unshakable determination and victory. It makes all the difference in the world.

Until I experienced it myself, I don't think I fully understood how families are

able to weather storms like life-threatening conditions. But as I tried to make sense of the chaos in my own life, I thought of Molly and the families that hers had befriended during the treatments. They were all ordinary people who were determined to fight something they couldn't control, and they showed extraordinary power by refusing to be beaten down by circumstances. My husband and I resolved that we would do the same. And as we spent time at the hospital and with support groups, we began to connect with other families just as Molly's family had, and the emotional assistance those families provided us was a tremendous encouragement. The messages of support that poured in from fans were humbling, as well. Just to know that many people are thinking of you and rooting for you—for something much bigger than a win on the links—is empowering. It reminds you to keep your focus and to keep on fighting even when you feel too exhausted to think.

I remember standing over the incubator one day, not long after Will was born, watching my tiny son struggling to live and thinking that it was all just too much. But then my mind flashed to Molly, laughing and smiling, enjoying life and loving to golf even as her body was fighting a terrible disease. I was shocked at myself. Why was I allowing negative thoughts to be so loud in my head? Why was I allowing myself to slip into patterns of defeatist thinking when I've always believed in mind over matter? I had seen firsthand that positive thinking defines a life far more than any kind of health challenge does. I simply had to embrace what I knew to be true and what I had seen Molly so clearly demonstrate: attitude is everything.

Of course, things don't always work out the way we planned, even if we do keep a good attitude about them. But that day with Molly illustrated more clearly than just about anything else in my life that old saying: "Life is 10 percent what happens to you and 90 percent what you make of it." Molly had decided to make something great out of her challenge. She had a fire to fight back and become even better at her game than before her diagnosis. So what was I going to make

of the difficult situation in which I was placed? I was going to take this shock lesson in perspective and reevaluate how I spent my time and energy to devote more to what really and truly matters to me. I was going to be thankful for every day that we had as a family, for every small bit of progress in Will's health, and for every chance we got to see him in the hospital. I decided it was going to make me a better mother to both my children, more patient with and grateful for them. I couldn't change the circumstances, but I could change my attitude.

In the fall of 2008, less than ten months after having her wish granted, Molly was back on the links for her high school team. She practiced diligently and helped her team finish their season undefeated and at the top of their league by forty strokes! Molly also qualified to compete in the state tournament as an individual, where she placed twelfth overall. Her sophomore season finish of eighty-nine was a full twenty-five strokes better than the previous year.

In early 2011, I received an e-mail from Molly, updating me on how she was doing. She finished her senior year of high school with a bang:

> I had four 1st place finishes, four 2nd place finishes, a 3rd, a 4th and a 6th. I finished with a season average of 77.2, which is 31 strokes better than my freshmen year average of 108. In four years I went from never breaking 100 to a career best 68 at the conference championship to tie the school record. To top it all off I was a unanimous pick to the all-state Super Team (which is the top eight girls in the state of Michigan). I have wanted this so badly and there is nothing like that feeling of knowing I have reached my goals.

Molly is now playing golf at Grand Valley State University, a women's golf powerhouse. Nowhere in her e-mail did she even mention her cancer; instead, she wrote like any enthusiastic young athlete excited about the next step in her career.

I can't begin to express the pride I have in her, as well as the hope that she gives me that health challenges do not have to define anyone's life. As a mother, it is such a relief to see that my family and my son do not have to have hospitals on our brains for the rest of our lives. Life is what you make it, and Molly has proven that she is so much more than her illness ever was.

Recently, I was asked to become an ambassador for Make-A-Wish, and I could not have been more honored. My motto is "share my passion," and that is exactly what I hope to achieve by working with Make-A-Wish—to help others share my passion for reaching out to children and families who deserve a little encouragement to keep up the fight.

The world of a professional athlete is full of distractions that make it easy to forget reality. When I was competing full-time, I was sometimes so focused on my schedule and my own concerns that I didn't always stop to put everything in its proper place. My work with Make-A-Wish has helped me to stay focused on what really matters. It has given me a sense of perspective that helps keep me grounded. After all, what is a bogey, really? What is shooting over par in the grand scheme of things? True, those things may be a big deal in my life, but not in the big picture. Meeting with children like Molly helps to remind me of the human side of things— that we are all in this life together and have an obligation to help one another out, to support each other, enjoy life, and make the most of it. Cherish what you have. Stay grounded. Don't take anything for granted. If you keep your mind focused on what really matters, nothing will seem like such a big deal that you can't overcome it.

THE GIFT OF MEMORIES

Scott Hamilton

My involvement with Make-A-Wish goes back about twenty-five years, so I've had the wonderful opportunity to meet countless children and grant many wishes during that time.

Sometimes I meet children who have just received a diagnosis; with those wishes, it is always so hard to think, "The next time I see this child, his or her life will have changed unimaginably." Sometimes, I meet children at the end of their battle, be that a clean bill of health after a tough fight or a letting go of this life and all the pain they had faced; being invited to be a part of their victories or working to bring the most joy possible into what little time is left is an incredible honor. Sometimes, the children with whom I interact are right in the middle of their treatment with the future uncertain but their determination pushing them forward.

Whenever I do a wish, whether it's as part of an ice skating show or exhibition, or even if we're just spending some one-on-one time together in the rink, the most common request I hear is "Do a back flip!" It was kind of my signature move for a while, so even though it never got me extra points in routines, I still liked to keep it a part of my repertoire of tricks because people seemed to love it. So when I got the request, I would always make sure to get as close as possible to where my wish kid was sitting at the rink and then flip. The look of excitement on their faces knowing that that flip belonged to them and no one else was just one of the greatest things in the world. All of my wish kids have amazed me in one way or another, but perhaps the one who best personified the spirit of all Make-A-Wish children was a tremendous little girl from Virginia named Krystal.

I first met Krystal for her wish at a skating rink in Richmond. It wasn't a large arena; instead, it was just a small ring of ice for doing birthday parties or promotions. When I first saw it, I'll admit that I was a little surprised at how small and seemingly unremarkable it was. I had thought we were going to be in a big rink that would really kind of re-create the feeling of skating in the Olympics or world championships, where there are thousands of seats in the audience and a huge sheet of ice out in front of you. And yet here I was in a small rink in Richmond, with really nothing especially impressive or exciting about it. It seemed strange to me that this could possibly be the setting for what was supposed to be one of the greatest days of a child's life. But looking back, I'll always remember it as a truly wonderful place because that was where I met the remarkably special little girl who would come to win my heart.

Krystal was seven years old and had been fighting to survive her entire life. In addition to a number of other health challenges, she had cerebral palsy and was dependent on a walker to move herself around. Everyone was nervous about having her out on the ice, where there are no railings to hold on to, and the walls that might offer support are awfully far apart. She was captivated by watching skaters on TV and wanted desperately to spin and leap alongside them, but her condition caused her feet to not point in the same direction, so it seemed like it might be impossible to make her wish come true. All the adults tried to dissuade her from trying to skate, and even I wondered at first if it was really a good idea, but Krystal would have no part of that. She wanted to be an ice skater. Nothing and no one was going to change her mind. I'll never forget: She had on a red polka-dot dress and red coat, with a matching red bow in her long hair. As her skates were laced up over her white tights, I asked her if she wanted help onto the ice, but she shook her head so that the bow swung side-to-side: "No, I'll do it myself."

And she did. It was unbelievable to see her push herself up to standing and then start out onto the ice, her walker sliding in front of her. There was a look on her face of pure determination mixed with unadulterated joy as she started to move. She never went very fast, but she was doing it on her own, and her immense pride was evident. My eyes teared up, and my throat felt about a mile thick. It was such a beautiful moment; I think everyone at the rink was overwhelmed by her joy.

For the next few years, Krystal became my East Coast buddy. At the time, I was touring with Stars on Ice, which benefited Make-A-Wish, and I don't think I had more loyal fans than Krystal and her parents, who came to just about every show that was anywhere nearby. From Hershey, Pennsylvania, to Norfolk, Virginia, they were there. I could always spot them down front, and I would wave to Krystal when I skated by; at the end of the show when the skaters would all come onto the ice together and then skate over to the stands to shake hands with the audience, I would always skate straight up to Krystal to give her a great big hug. She gave the greatest hugs in the world—that's something else I will never forget about her—and she would tell me about her favorite parts of the show. Afterward, I would wait backstage for her family so I could spend more time with them. It was always quite an undertaking to get Krystal to the shows, because she had to be hooked up to several machines to keep her body functioning properly. They would be running on battery power during the performance, so she would have to get plugged back in to recharge after an outing like that. But I didn't care how long I had to wait: if someone was going to travel that far and go through that much just to cheer me on, I was going to make time for her.

Because of her irresistible smile and her wonderful personality, Krystal became one of the Make-A-Wish poster children for her area. I always got a rush of pride when I saw her featured in an advertisement or announcement for the organization. "She's one of mine!" I wanted to say to anyone who would listen. Krystal was also befriended by a local news personality, who included her in covering some stories around the Richmond area. You just couldn't be around that little girl without falling in love with her, and everyone who met her wanted to do something to honor her amazing courage and million-dollar smile.

Beyond just seeing them at Stars on Ice performances, I also formed a friendship with the Williams family outside of the rink. For the next six years, if her treatment was in a place where she couldn't make my show in her area, I would go and visit Krystal in the hospital. For a while, her two favorite people in the world were me and Billy Ray Cyrus, and she had a photo collage posted in her room of the two of us alongside pictures of her new kitten. She would always tell me proudly about the new pictures she'd cut out from newspapers or magazines of Billy Ray and me, or she'd talk about what her cat was up to as it got bigger and bigger. It was always tough to see her in the hospital, knowing what she was going through—what her whole family was going through. Krystal's condition was so serious that she needed to undergo a transplant of an unbelievable seven vital organs simultaneously—*and* have them all successfully adapt to her body—to even have a shot at reaching adulthood. As you can imagine, the odds of that happening were bleak, for a number of reasons. She'd already undergone the surgery twice, but both times one or more of the organs were rejected by her body, a terribly painful process for anyone but especially for a small child. But Krystal soldiered on.

One day before a show in Hershey, I was so happy to see Krystal in the audience, because I knew she had been going through a particularly rough period of treatments. I asked her how she was doing. "I'm okay," she said. "But I don't think I want to do the surgeries anymore."

I was shocked. "But why?"

She answered very matter-of-factly. "It makes my mother sad."

I didn't know how to respond except to say, selfishly, "But I want you here for the rest of a long life."

Krystal shook her head. "My mom would never show it, but it makes her so sad when I go through all this, and it doesn't work."

I was utterly floored. It was so incredible to me that an elementary school–aged child could not only be so perceptive and so selfless but also be so wise and accepting of such a situation. It was all I could do to keep my composure during the rest of the preshow warm-up. Russian gold medalist Katia Gordeeva skated up to me a few minutes later and asked, "Who is that beautiful little girl you were talking to?" When I told her about Krystal, Katia said with real compassion, "Is she going to be okay?" I almost broke down crying as I told her, "I don't think so."

Not long after that, I was diagnosed with cancer, and my whole life changed. I began to understand just how truly draining, both physically and emotionally, it is to be in and out of hospitals, waiting for test results to come back, trying to read the doctors' faces as they go over charts. After what seemed like endless months of treatments and an uncertain prognosis, I was finally well enough to take a long drive out west to clear my mind and do some thinking and praying about what I wanted the next phase of my life to look like. I intentionally took myself off the grid to just have some restorative time to myself, so I was avoiding e-mail and my phone and anything else that might have pulled me out of the moment. For that reason, it wasn't until the end of that trip that I learned that Krystal, my sweet, beautiful, tremendously brave Krystal, had passed away the week before.

I feel like I always carry her with me, now. I have a picture of that first day on skates that I absolutely treasure and always have handy whenever I need to remind myself of how incredibly precious life is. Every time someone comes into your life, they leave a little mark on you. Everyone affects us; every meeting changes us somehow in ways that we can reference later. Krystal's mark on my life is one that I find myself referencing often. She reminds me all the time about the fact that we are all in this crazy life together. We need to see that we are all here to support one another. Everyone has a different story; our challenges are all different. For some people, those challenges are minimal while for others, they are profound. But they are all real, and we all need to be willing to help one another through them.

Make-A-Wish is such a beautiful organization because their mission is so significant in how it honors the tremendous bravery of some of the most remarkable people among us.

In 1990, I had the incredible honor of being named Make-A-Wish's first-ever "Celebrity Wish Granter of the Year." We're told, as skaters, that the audience always feels more engaged in a performance if you include them in what you are doing. Therefore, it is important to look out into the crowd, make eye contact with people, and make sure that folks feel like they are a part of your experience as much as you are a part of theirs. I think back to times I've been at concerts and one of the artists would look out into the crowd. If I felt like he or she made eye contact with me, it made the whole concert seem more personal and meaningful because I had just been pulled into the performer's world for a little bit. That's what I try to accomplish when I engage with people on the ice, and I think in some ways that is the perfect metaphor for what Krystal taught me about life. It's far too easy to just go about our jobs, focused only on whatever our next hurdle is and not really paying attention to the lives and the stories of the people who surround us. But if you occasionally look around and interact with people, even in just a small way, it can completely change the experience.

We all want a life filled with wonderful memories of moments that made us feel loved, feel special, feel like we were accomplishing something just by being who we are. Make-A-Wish children are no different from you and me; they want those very same things, and it is within the power of any of us and all of us to make it happen.

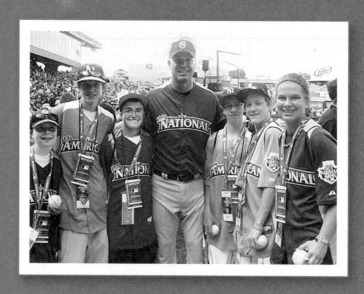

RISING TO
THE CHALLENGE

Chipper Jones

I was still pretty new to the big leagues, in my second or third season, and I was invited to something called the Buckmaster Classic outside of Selma, Alabama. It was a pretty neat time to be at the Buckmaster, since there were all kinds of sports figures there—like Wade Boggs (who was with the Yankees at the time); Curt Hennig, the wrestler; and a number of other guys from the Atlanta Braves.

There also happened to be a Make-A-Wish kid there, whose wish had nothing at all to do with me but was instead there just to hang out at the camp and enjoy the outdoors. (While Make-A-Wish no longer grants hunting wishes, this was back in the mid-1990s when they still occasionally did.) And that was how I got to meet Matthew.

He was only eleven years old at the time and was fighting a life-threatening respiratory condition, but he had such an incredible sparkle in his eyes. (I would see later that this is a common thing among Make-A-Wish kids who have fought back against all they've had to face.) He actually walked right up to me—I hadn't introduced myself or anything—and said, "Mr. Jones, I was hunting a piece of property you were hunting today, and I saw a monster. I really want you to harvest that deer because I'd like to see him. I'd like to put my hands on him."

There was something about his request that I just couldn't say no to. We made a little wager and I said, "You know what, Matthew? I'm going to bring him back to camp and let you hang on to him." And surprisingly enough, I was able to find that same huge buck he described, and I ended up harvesting him. When we brought him back to camp and pulled down the tailgate, Matthew took one look at that deer and, with tears in his eyes, said to me, "I knew you were going to get him." He was so genuinely happy for me, and we formed a friendship right then and there.

About two months after the Classic, he relapsed and went into the hospital. His wish was to harvest a deer and have it mounted so he could hang it in his room. Jackie Bushman, the coordinator of the Buckmaster Classic, put a rush order on the buck I had harvested, and they were able to present it to Matthew right there as he lay in his hospital bed. His face lit up, and he took that mount and just gave it a giant bear hug. Only about an hour or two later, Matthew passed away hugging that deer.

That experience was the one that got me absolutely hooked on being a part of granting wishes. Even though Matthew's wish had not actually involved me, I was so excited to get to be a part of bringing some joy to a sick kid who just wanted to experience a little more in life before his time was up. I've been very lucky. Within my family, there are no major illnesses. I still have all my grandparents, and I still have my parents. I've never had to deal with the loss of a family member or, really, go through anything serious. That was the first time something tragic really hit close to home for me.

Since then, I've been privileged to be a part of more wishes than I can count. Sometimes, the wish is specifically to hang out with me; other times, it's a more general wish about going to a Braves game. The first time the Braves approached me about a Make-A-Wish kid whose specific request was to meet me, I was flabbergasted. I said, "Are you kidding me? His one wish was to come here and meet me?" I couldn't understand why he'd want to do that, but when I walked through the door to greet him, his face lit up and I could have sworn he was about to jump out of that wheelchair. I had a blast that day, and once again, I was totally blown away by the twinkle in that kid's eyes that said, "I am more than my disease."

Actually, on second thought, it's more than just a twinkle in the eyes—it's more like a fire in the belly. And I figure that if, somewhere along the line, I can provide even a little bit of encouragement, I want to give it everything I've got. I have been blessed with the fact that I can hit a baseball better than most people; it's not the greatest talent in the world, but it's what I have. From the point of view of a professional athlete, it's really easy to take for granted the sport that you play. You think that people just turn on the TV and watch you play. You don't really realize the effect that you have on them, and that your personality comes through, and that people can actually get excited about you through the TV, or become connected to you because you have something in common. Or perhaps they watch you do an interview and like your philosophy on the game or on life or whatever, or perhaps you just make a flat-out good play that impresses people. The point is, a lot of times professional athletes don't really realize the effect that we have on people. And if who I am, how I play, and what I stand for mean a lot to someone—especially a little kid who has been dealt such a rough hand—I feel like I have a responsibility to use that skill to lift someone up.

Beyond the kids, it's amazing to see what an impact you can have on the families, too. You see how tired they all are, worn out by hospital visits and constant worry. It makes you hurt inside. It really does. You almost feel undeserving of the advantages that you've been given in your lifetime when somebody else has had to suffer so much. And that's why I want to be positive and lift everyone's spirits as much as possible. If I'm upbeat toward the kids, then the families are in turn going to be lifted up as well. They have a lot of that roller coaster–type life where they don't know when they wake up in the morning if today's going to be a good day or a bad day. I want to do whatever I can to make sure that their day with me is a good day—one of their family's best.

I haven't had the opportunity to include my sons on any of my wishes because those events are usually last minute. The team's schedule is so hectic, and we're traveling around almost daily. I'll usually hear around 2:00 P.M., "We have a Make-A-Wish kid coming in this afternoon, and she's going to be out on the field," or "We're going to bring him by the clubhouse," or whatever the case may be. But even though

my sons haven't had the opportunity to see a wish granted firsthand, they hear me talk about it *all the time*. I try to stress to them the fact that nothing is certain, so they need to put everything into each and every day because you don't know when some life-altering illness is going to show up in your life, or if an accident might change your abilities. We've seen so many lives altered over the course of the years. I've met kids who have been completely healthy but then suddenly impacted by a life-threatening illness, and now their Make-A-Wish experience is to come see me, even as they struggle to adjust to a new way of life. It rips your heart out to hear of what these kids are facing. I try to focus on that when I tell my sons that nothing is guaranteed—your health can be taken from you tomorrow. You might think, "That would never happen to me," but it happens to people every day. And it never fails to amaze me how resilient so many of those kids are—even the ones who know that they aren't going to ever recover. Their life has absolutely been turned inside out, but they keep fighting anyway, as long as they can, trying to get the absolute most they can out of life.

I'm not going to lie, though—it is scary sometimes. I always worry a little that I may say the wrong thing or do something that makes them feel uncomfortable. It's funny that I don't feel nervous on the baseball field with millions of people watching, but I do when talking to a little kid. I don't always know that I'm going to say the right things. I don't know that I'm going to actually be able to make this kid feel better. You have to remember that these kids probably look forward to this day for weeks and weeks, and you want to make it the most special day possible.

We had one young man named Noah, from Iowa, whose wish was to attend a game and talk to the players in the locker room. I got to spend a little one-on-one time with him, and I could tell he was as nervous as I was. The last thing I wanted to happen was for him to go away from that experience thinking, "Wow. I got to meet Chipper Jones, but we didn't really talk to each other." So I tried to crack a couple jokes just to break the ice, and that was really all it took. It helped me to see how important it is to bring that kind of levity to wishes. It's great when we have Make-A-Wish kids come into the clubhouse, because it eliminates a lot of that awkwardness when you first meet of wondering what to say or how to start that engagement with each other. I mean, what more awesome way is there to kind of break the ice than to be hanging out in a major league clubhouse! There are shenanigans galore going on in major league clubhouses pretty much all the time. You sit there long enough and you're going to laugh out loud at something. We're all so glad to see the kids, and the laughter just catches on. They see that we're normal people, just like them, and it's just such a great experience to all be laughing together. It makes them feel like part of the team, like they're surrounded by friends.

Have you ever seen a kids on Christmas morning and how they light up? Have twenty-five major league ballplayers from the Atlanta Braves come up and give a kid who's a Braves fan some batting gloves or a pair of cleats—just little mementoes from their visit here—and you can't replace the look on their face. They are laughing and grinning from ear to ear. It's magical. They say that laughter is the best medicine, and I think there's some truth to that. Even if it's just emotional healing, I think that being able to break through the nervousness—for all of us—and being able to just enjoy some relaxed, happy time together does tremendous things for everyone's spirits.

Of course, I sometimes get nervous all over again when a kid asks me to hit a home run for him or her during the game. I always promise I'll do my best, but I hate that I'm not always able to deliver. I don't want any child to feel like their day was less than perfect because I wasn't able to hold up my end of the deal. I did have one kid say, "I don't want you to hit a home run; I want you to hit two." Talk about pressure! But you know what? That was a game when I did manage to hit two homers. It was probably the most surreal moment of my career because I rounded first on the first one, and I just kind of chuckled to myself, thinking this kid must think it is the most unbelievable thing in the world—that I actually managed to hit one for him. But the second time, well, let's just say that it must have been divine intervention. From the moment I made contact, I just knew it. I knew it was gone from the time I hit it. I just stood there at home plate, and I really hoped that the pitcher wasn't thinking I was showing him up, but I couldn't tear my eyes away from that ball. I was absolutely in awe. Finally, I managed to make myself start running, and I remember thinking, "Thank you, Lord. I appreciate that. I *needed* that." It didn't just make that kid's night, but it also showed me that God was working. I had been feeling kind of down, and I think I needed that to get me back on track spiritually. It took everything I had not to get misty-eyed as I crossed home plate.

I would just like to take this opportunity to speak to all professional athletes who might be reading this book: we are role models, whether we like it or not, and we have the ability to do some pretty special things if we put out a little effort. These kids put so much hope and excitement into whether we win or lose, and we have a chance to provide some healing power just by giving our time to these kids. I urge you to get out there and take advantage of every opportunity possible. It's such a privilege to know that we can contribute, even in a small and seemingly insignificant way, to someone's healing process. What an honor!

My teammates sometimes joke that I would grant a wish every single day if I could. The thing is, they're right. I get such a sense of fulfillment from it that I kind of feel a little selfish about saying that, but it's true. The best way I can describe it is, as a veteran baseball player, it's like mentoring a younger teammate who's in a slump. You give him a tip or a nugget of information, and then you watch him go out and have success on the field. He looks back at you with a look that says, "Got it." You're in the game together, both cheering on the other's success as you work toward the same goal. It's the same thing with Make-A-Wish kids. You walk in and you lock eyes with them, and for that first second, you can see that they are tough but tired. But then that all goes away and you see the excitement and the determination, and it's just awesome. If I can grant somebody that feeling just because I play baseball, I'd do it every day. I'd do it twenty times a day because there's nothing that can replace that. Nothing.

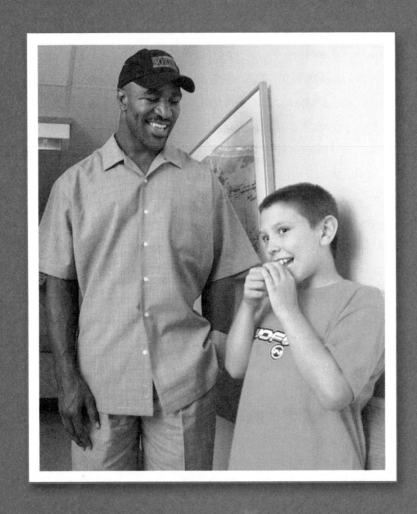

WISHES ARE PART
OF A MISSION

Evander Holyfield

I am a praying man. Every morning and
before every event, I always hit my knees and
spend a little time talking with God.

The same is true before I participate in any wish. I always try to spend a little time in prayer before I go visit a sick child and his or her family. There is no question that I will participate—of course I will. What I am praying about is how to best encourage the child and his or her family, and how to give them hope, strength, and faith for the future.

It's tough to know how to feel when you find out that you've been requested by a child to grant a wish. On the one hand, I want to be excited for them that they are able to have their wish granted (and that I get to be a part of it), but on the other hand, I'm obviously really sad for them and the situation they're facing. Most of all, though, I think I have a very serious feeling of having a mission to bring the child and his or her family a sense of peace, hope, and closure. The peace comes from them knowing that someone who has never even met them cares about them and is praying for them. The hope comes from the thought that, "I had a wish come true when Evander showed up! I wonder what other good things can happen?" And the closure comes from knowing either that the worst of the treatments is over and the healing process can start, or that the child had a big day that made them feel special and happy before they pass on.

I think that last part—the feeling of being able to bring closure—was especially true when I granted one wish for a seventeen-year-old boy in Maine named Ben. He was in a coma following surgery to remove a brain tumor, and his family asked Make-A-Wish if I could come up to see him, even though he wouldn't know I was there, because Ben had been a boxer and they knew that a visit with me would have been very special to him. Again, it was a situation where I was happy to help, but I was also so sad that the situation existed at all. It was tough, and I really felt for the family. But I did go up to Portland, and I spent several hours in the hospital, taking pictures with the family, talking, and sharing stories with them. They told me all about Ben—his boxing, his goals, and some of his matches. I told them some boxing stories of my own. But I think the most important thing we did was when we just sat together and prayed for strength and peace in the difficult days that lay ahead for them. It was tough, but it was also very uplifting for all of us. I was so touched by the family's amazing love for Ben, and I believe the family was encouraged by the fact that someone their son cared about was willing to reach out to them.

My goal with any wish, as it was with Ben's wish, is to try to let God shine through me to the people I meet. I'm a Christian and a man of faith. It's impossible to separate my message from the person I am, so I have come to view these wishes as a chance to take God to people who are hurting. They want to meet me because of my career, but I want to meet them to bring them something much more important than some boxing titles: hope. It's become part of my personal mission. If the child and the family already have faith, then we can celebrate that together. If not, I hope that I can share with them that essential part of who I am simply by extending to them the grace and love that God has shown me.

Usually during a wish, someone will ask me, "Is boxing really as tough as it looks on TV?" My answer is, "Yes," and then I talk about the discipline required for training and how you have to control your mind in the ring and not think about the pain of the punches. But after that, I try to add something more meaningful. "Life itself is tough," I tell them. "Life is going to throw you punches and try to knock you down or knock you out. You certainly know that, given everything your family is up against right now. But whatever I'm going through, whether it's stepping into the ring or stepping up to fight against challenges in life, I know that everything is ultimately going to be okay. Because of my faith, I know that there is more to life than just what is right in front of me at this moment, and in the end, it's all going to be all right. Not everything will go your way. Not every call will go in your favor, and you can't deflect or avoid every punch, but if you have faith, you can rest assured that God is in control."

It's a good message for me to hear, too. Sharing my beliefs with other families reminds me of the work I want to be doing with my own. It's so important to make sure that our public lives and our private lives are consistent, and in either one we never lose sight of what really matters. My time with wish children always helps to remind me of that, and I try to carry those lessons with me when I leave the hospital room or the family's house. Sometimes, the things we do as an extension of our careers have a big impact on the way we live our lives at home, and that's definitely true for me with regard to granting wishes. I believe that for my words to ring true for the children whose wishes I am granting, I have to really be living by them in my own life, and a big part of that starts by what I talk to my own kids about at home.

There was no dad in my home growing up, so now I feel the extreme importance of making sure that my presence is clear in my children's lives. A big part of that is making sure that they are hearing the right messages. That's something we should care about for all children. I know that firsthand, and I know that I only got to where

I am today because certain people cared enough to invest some time in me, so I hope that I am able to do the same for others. But that's not just true for me. It's true for all of us. We're all where we are because somebody took a little bit or a lot of time to help our minds and our hearts and our souls grow.

To me, the message of faith in God is something that my mama taught me and my grandmother taught her; so when I share it with my kids, I am really just passing on a lesson that someone else gave me. I'm not doing anything new or teaching anything that came out of my own wisdom. Any lesson I share with a wish child is one I shared with my own children first, and one that was shared with me by someone who loved and cared about me when I was younger. In that way, I think we can all have a part in granting wishes. Promoting at home the good, positive things that we believe can carry us through the trials of life and allow us to grow stronger in that message so that we can then carry it out into the world to impact other people. Those words of hope never grow old. That wisdom never loses its importance. Those lessons are timeless. In fact, they often reach people at just the right time . . . as long as we are willing to share them.

Each wish is different because every child, every family, and every situation is different. But I hope that I can accomplish the same thing with all of them. My prayer with all the wishes I grant is that God will use me in whatever way he wants to reach that family with whatever message will help them the most. The day isn't about me, but I want to be the best possible instrument for good that I can be while I have the opportunity with that special child and their family.

The way I see it, we're all put on this earth to help each other out. That's ultimately our job here. The more you are sought out to help, the more responsibility you have to keep doing good. If someone wants to meet me because of my God-given boxing talents, then that is part of my job, my mission—to meet with them and maybe help them through one of the toughest things they will probably ever have to face in life. My skills aren't my own; my fame isn't my own. That all comes from God. So if those things matter to someone else and I can help encourage that person in some way because of those gifts, then I am happy to do whatever I can. Making wishes come true is part of my mission, and it's a mission I am very happy to have.

ONE PERSON CAN
MAKE A DIFFERENCE—
A CHILD CHANGED ME

Larry Fitzgerald

*At the past Make-A-Wish Ball, I was strolling through the silent
auction items and looking at the various offerings, trying to figure out what
I wanted to bid on, when there was suddenly a little tug on my sleeve.*

I was surprised that someone might be trying to get my attention, since I didn't really know anyone there. I wasn't a formally invited guest myself, but my friend Steven Ellman (who serves on the board for the local chapter of Make-A-Wish) knew of my love for the foundation and asked if I'd like to come along. So I turned around (a little confused) to see who was pulling on my sleeve, and there stood Jordan. He was a little taller than when I'd first met him, and when he said hello, I could tell that he was speaking a little more clearly, but it was definitely and unmistakably my little buddy Jordan.

I first met Jordan a year before, when he was four. He loves watching sports, and his wish was to meet me, so he and his family were invited down to the Arizona Cardinals' training facility in Tempe to watch a practice and hang out with me afterward. He was absolutely grinning the entire time, holding a big bunch of balloons from Make-A-Wish that seemed to dwarf such a tiny guy. His parents and his brother were with him as well, and even though Jordan seemed a little unsure or overwhelmed at first, his dad held his hand the whole time, and you could tell that they were both pretty excited about his special day. The whole family seemed to be enjoying the time away from the hospital, sitting together and just having fun as if, for that one day, they didn't have any other cares in the world.

As soon as practice was over, I brought about ten of my teammates over with me to say hello and meet the family. It was the coolest thing. Before I knew it, everyone was talking and laughing, and the Cardinals who had joined us were taking off gloves to give to the boys. I signed a pair of shoes and then took a practice ball—and Jordan—and went down to the locker room to get the ball auto-graphed by more players and coaches, and to show Jordan around our facilities. You wouldn't believe how tiny he looked in the midst of all those huge football players, but everyone was so gentle and funny with him that we were soon all laughing and high-fiving each other as if he were part of the defensive line. We talked about what he was learning in preschool and what kinds of games he liked to play with his brother and his friends. I tried to make sure that we steered clear of his illness unless he brought it up; I didn't want him to feel like he had to talk about it unless he wanted to.

At home, I keep a framed picture of his family as a reminder of that great day, so to see him and his family again at the ball was such a wonderful surprise. Jordan looked healthy and happy (which was the best part of all). I kneeled down and started talking to him, telling him he cleaned up really well and that, thanks to him and his dapper little tux, I was no longer the best-dressed man in the room. He started grinning his fantastic little grin again, just beaming from ear to ear. His whole family was there, so I was able to catch up with all of them and hear about how Jordan's recovery was progressing. That was absolutely the highlight of my evening and kept *me* grinning nonstop for at least the next week.

I had no idea when I first started working with Make-A-Wish how much I would be changed by each experience. I remember before I got to the NFL watching segments on TV about athletes granting wishes, and I always thought it sounded like such an amazing thing to help a sick child live out a dream, but I didn't understand that being part of that could shift your whole paradigm. Fast-forward a few years, and there I was, playing in the NFL just like the guys I used to watch, when Make-A-Wish reached out to me with Jordan's story and wish. I was shocked at first, because I always figured it was big celebrities who got these kinds of requests.

Of course I was eager to help out and incredibly honored that Jordan would have chosen me to be part of his wish, but I didn't realize how changed I would be at the end of the day.

My first thought after learning about his situation and meeting his family was "Wow! Those parents are so strong." My own son was two years old at the time, and I remember arriving home after practice that day and getting on my knees, thanking the Lord that my son was healthy. It gives you a sense of gratitude for the little trials and stresses of your day—that the worst you may have to deal with is a fussy child with teething pains or a stomach bug or anything else temporary and minor. Of course, no parent likes to see their child suffer, but sometimes it's easy to get wrapped up in thinking about the inconveniences you have to face ("I only got three hours of sleep last night because my child

kept waking up with an earache") instead of counting your blessings ("Thank goodness it was only an earache"). That night after meeting Jordan, I realized that I could not care less what my son decides to be when he grows up. I don't care where he decides to go to college. I don't care about how he wears his hair. Provided that he is growing to be a healthy young man who makes good decisions, knows he is loved, and is happy, I have absolutely no room to complain. It's amazing how quickly all the other little worries of life fall by the wayside when you realize what truly matters and what a gift you have really been given with a healthy child.

It's also surprising how much you find yourself wanting to talk about the wish-granting experience after you've been a part of it. I couldn't wait to tell friends about the amazing little kid I'd met and his fantastic family. I felt so moved to share

that experience with my family, my teammates, and anyone else who I thought might listen because I wanted them to jump on the opportunity immediately if they ever had a chance to participate. There are so many ways to get involved, and I really believe that once someone participates, he or she will never regret it and will be eager to participate again. Just think about how you feel inside when you're able to make a child smile . . . and then multiply that by a thousand.

That night when I was a guest at the Wish Ball, I realized that I wanted to make a lifelong commitment to the foundation. Looking around the room and seeing all the other people who were partners in this fantastic effort really gave me a sense of purpose—I wanted to be a staunch supporter in whatever way I could. And then being spotted by Jordan again? That sealed the deal for me. I will forever be grateful to Jordan for making that wish and allowing me the chance to meet him and gain a whole new perspective on things. It changed me forever as an athlete, as a dad, and as a person.

EVERY CHILD DESERVES

A CHILDHOOD

Jim Kleinsasser

For me, it all started with meeting kids on the sidelines at games.

We'd be warming up, getting ready to play, and then someone

would come up with a cute kid in a Vikings jersey (or, more likely,

bundled up with a purple-and-gold scarf, gloves, and earmuffs) and

we'd shake hands, take some photos, and talk with the child.

They always seemed so excited to be there and so tiny—even the teenagers—in the midst of all those NFL players. It was impossible not to feel your heart melt a little when you learned that they were from Make-A-Wish and that this trip to the game and chat with the players was one bright spot in the midst of their hospital stays, treatments, and uncertain futures.

In fact, I remember one game where a girl who needed a kidney transplant had wished to do the coin toss. So out onto the field walks this beautiful little girl with such a strong look on her face—as if she knew everything she was going to have to deal with during her treatment and recovery but was ready to take it on—and after she flipped the coin, she went skipping off of the field. Right then and there, I thought, "Any worries I have about playing the game, they're nothing. That little girl is facing a way bigger game against way bigger opponents, and she's still managing to skip and smile." I remember that I was standing next to Bubby Brister, who had two little girls himself, and he said something along the lines of, "You know what? I'm not really that sore today, after all. I can't really be complaining." And he was absolutely right. It was one of those moments that just puts everything into perspective for the people present. It's funny that a group of big, mean football players found strength from the example of a little girl, but that's the power of watching wishes be granted. And I knew right away I wanted to start helping out Make-A-Wish. What I didn't know right away was just how large a part of my life wish granting would become.

As a kid from Carrington, North Dakota, who had the honor of playing football for the team I grew up cheering for, I think it was especially easy for the kids to connect with me since I sound more like a hometown guy and could talk with them about hockey or snowmobiling or sledding or ice fishing or any of the other things that kids from the upper Midwest love that guys from, say, Texas or Florida might not know about in the same way. But for my wife, Christa, and me, our interaction with Make-A-Wish has not been so much granting wishes in the traditional sense—as in, a child wants to meet me so we spend an afternoon hanging out. I'd be more than happy to meet those requests, but there aren't that many specifically targeting me. Instead, we've dedicated ourselves to trying to make wishes come true by sponsoring them or supporting fundraisers that increase awareness and generate resources for helping out kids and their families. Recently, there was a four-year-old cancer patient named Kaden who loves boats and boating with his family, so he made a wish to "go on a really big boat!" The logical way to grant that wish was to send them all on a cruise. Two wonderful women, Kim De Keyrel and Krista Ryan, coordinated a golf tournament and silent auction for Make-A-Wish in Rochester, Minnesota, and Kaden was the centerpiece of the event. They presented the family with the cruise at the banquet dinner following the tournament. It was a really neat experience for us to feel like we were directly contributing to someone else's happiness, and a great reminder of what a unique position we are in to be able to help people.

When I had the honor of being involved in the wish for that little boy who wanted a cruise, I really felt the gut punch of that pain when I realized that the bright, bubbly, energetic little boy shared the same name as my younger son, Cayden. (My older son is Carter.) Somehow, it just made me feel more than ever that but for the grace of God, that could be my family. To see his family so appreciative, warm, and so determined to make the day all about their little guy and celebrating his bravery really made me admire their strength and wonder if I could bring the same positive attitude to the situation if it were me watching one of my own children face something so rough.

My wife has actually been the real champ of all of this. In 2008, she served as the co-chair for the annual Wish Ball, a black-tie event held in the Twin Cities to help raise funds for the Minnesota chapter of Make-A-Wish. It is a huge event involving live entertainment, gourmet food, and silent auctions to help raise funds for the foundation. People from all over the state come out for it, and Minnesota athletes and other stars donate their time to help bring attention to the work the foundation does. Vikings linebacker Chad Greenway got involved with the Wish Ball a few years ago and, along with his own foundation, has continued to support Make-A-Wish. In fact, a number of my teammates have been enthusiastic about pitching in to make a difference.

I am a huge fan of fishing, so for two years in a row, I auctioned off a day of fishing with me where afterward I would make dinner. I figured that a couple of big football fans would be the ones to buy that; instead, the auction was won by Chad and two other Vikings, Ben Leber and John Sullivan. Together with their wives, they bid on it and ended up having a great time fishing and letting me cook for them afterward. And the Wish Ball grows each year. In 2012, the event hosted more than nine hundred people and included the wonderful opportunity for one little girl named Kennedy to dance with the city ballet company in Saint Paul. Kennedy missed her first dance recital because of treatments for Landau-Kleffner syndrome, a form of epilepsy. Kennedy was so excited to perform with professional ballerinas, and the guests had the chance to see the impact of a wish in action.

We've also been involved with Stories of Light and Delicious Wishes, which are other Make-A-Wish-themed events. Stories of Light was a Christmastime tradition in the Twin Cities, and it was actually my first fundraising event for Make-A-Wish. People or companies can sponsor a nighttime light display in a building downtown and that, in turn, helps to sponsor a wish for a child. During his rookie year, Adrian Peterson went out to the shopping mall in Bloomington with me to sign autographs as part of the publicity for that event. Now, Make-A-Wish of Minnesota does Season of Wishes, with next year's goal being forty wishes during the holiday season. It is such an exciting and meaningful effort. And Delicious Wishes? Well, that one is just a lot of fun for anyone who loves to eat—like football players! Usually held in the fall, it brings together some of the top chefs in the area for a casual evening of sampling various dishes and desserts, and even giving some cooking demonstrations and tips.

Sometimes I feel a little guilty that the sports figures are the ones that often get the headlines at these events when the truth is that there are dozens of people in the organization and volunteers who have put in countless hours and untold amounts of energy into making the evening happen who really deserve the thanks and credit. That's one of the reasons I was so excited to be voted onto the board of directors for the Make-A-Wish chapter of Minnesota in the summer of 2012. Here was my chance to not just participate in the "fun stuff" of fundraising and granting wishes but to really invest myself in the heavy lifting and the nitty-gritty details that make it all possible. There is so much that goes on behind the scenes for every wish and every event that is never seen, and the folks who really pull everything together and make it all possible are kind of invisible. As I write this, I'm still learning the ropes, since my election is still very new. I will be starting out by serving on the program committee, which will give me a pretty good overview of the organization and will help show me how everything fits together. I'm hoping that once I learn a little more I will be able to bring in some of my football connections and friends from the outdoors business to help bring in further support for wishes from the various relationships and networks in my own life.

The thing about it is, every child deserves a childhood. Every kid deserves a chance to feel normal, to not be worried about heavy stuff, to just enjoy being innocent and happy. That's not to say that wish kids aren't able to be happy, but they need a break from all that they're going through to just enjoy some carefree time with their family like other kids have. I consider it one of the greatest honors of my life that I have been given the opportunity to work with such a wonderful organization and to have been elected to serve on its board. Wishes give everyone a little bit of a lift, from the child and his or her family to the volunteers who help put on events or contribute to wishes. That's why I want to applaud anyone who purchased this book, as well, because you are now a wish granter, too, since the proceeds from this book return to Make-A-Wish to help them continue their important work. I hope that fills you with a sense of pride and purpose, because you have done a great thing by showing your interest in and support and encouragement for thousands of seriously ill children.

Thank you.

IT'S ABOUT DOING RIGHT

Ricky Carmichael

Ever since I was a kid, my parents stressed to me the importance

of doing right by people with special needs or particularly difficult

circumstances. I have two cousins who faced life-changing health

conditions, so learning to adapt and making sure to reach out to folks

has been a part of my everyday life for as long as I can remember.

Once I grew up and started racing motocross, I began to have requests to grant wishes for seriously ill children as part of Make-A-Wish, and it was just the most natural fit in the world. In fact, wishes undoubtedly rank among the very top things that I love about my job and the blessings it has brought to my life.

My goal with every wish is to overdeliver. I think a lot of families assume that our meeting will be short, since I'm getting ready for a race: just a couple of pictures and a handshake. But I want every family to look back on their time with my team and me and think, "What a wonderful, *wonderful* day!" I want them to feel like they got everything they possibly could out of their day at the race and their time with me. That's a little tough, since I have to be gone for part of the time because I'm racing, but I remember my cousins and the challenges they faced, and I know that I need to make the most of the opportunity I have to show these kids how special they are and what an honor it is for me to be a part of their wishes.

Before the races, I like to sit down with the kids and spend some time just talking, getting to know them, and hanging out. I know some athletes prefer to have their meetings with wish kids on days when they aren't competing or maybe after the game because they are afraid that they might get too emotional, which would break their concentration. Everyone has to do what they have to do, but I, for one, love meeting with kids ahead of my races. I'm able to be a regular person, stay relaxed, and keep focused on real life instead of just the race. For me, it's not about getting into "the zone" but about keeping my mind attuned to what really matters instead of falling into the trap of thinking that my performance that day is the be-all and end-all of life.

If the kids want to sit on the bike, that's great. I'll plop them up on the seat and show them all the different gears and gauges, or we'll look at my uniform or helmet. Whatever they want to do, I try to make it happen for them. A lot of kids are shy at first, so I find the best way to get past that is simply to show them that I am exactly like them, except that I ride motorcycles (and now race trucks) for a living. I give them hugs and high fives, crack jokes, or do whatever else will make them feel like they're getting a visit from a goofy big brother rather than a sports figure. After all, I'm just a kid from Tallahassee, Florida, who loves to goof off and compete in what I love. There is nothing fancy about me, so there is no need to worry about saying or doing the wrong thing.

Nervousness is the last thing I want them to feel on their wish day! Before I have to go to race, I make sure that they have a Ricky Carmichael jersey, and I also stress to the family that if they need anything at all—drinks, food, a place to cool off—they should just give my guys a holler and we'll make it happen. We always have a tent set up next to the big rig with all our equipment, so I make sure that they know that they have a cool place to go and sit and get whatever they might want or need. I always tell them, "You're part of the team today, so make yourself at home."

I've got to say, too, that my team is always so great at taking care of the kids and their families while I'm busy racing. Two people in particular, Mike Gosselaar and Tony Berluti, are especially great. They are both mechanics and can answer any question kids might have about the bikes. How often do you have to change the tires? How do the engines work? If the kids are curious, Mike and Tony will spend as much time as it takes to explain everything in terms they can grasp. I just love that the whole team is so invested in making the entire day special for wish kids. They get that that is part of the team's mission as much as helping me prep for a race. We're all in this together, and I am so lucky to have them as a part of what I do.

After the race, I try to make sure that I am able to spend some more time together with my special guests, discussing their favorite parts of the day, going over what they thought about the race and whatever else they might want to talk about. My goal is to make sure that they have a whole-day experience, even during the times that I can't be right there with them. I just really want to make sure that they have a great time, creating memories together and feeling special for a day, enjoying time with no treatments, no hospitals, and no worries. Ideally, when it's all said and done, I want them to think of Ricky Carmichael and the crew as their buddies before they think of us as a race team. If we accomplish that, then I think we've done it right.

Sometimes you're just so impressed by the strength and determination of the kids. Sometimes you leave with a sense of wanting to change your own outlook and perspective on life. Sometimes, especially after meeting with kids who look perfectly healthy on the outside but are actually battling terrible illnesses, you are reminded that you never really know what someone has going on and what invisible battles they might be fighting. It's a powerful reminder to try to be kind to everyone and not make judgments about a person based simply on what you think you can tell about them from their appearance.

Every wish has affected me in some way and made me a better person for having had that interaction. I remember that there was one wish where a boy with a life-threatening medical condition who had lost his sight in a motorcycle crash wanted to meet me. He had loved racing and was getting into it as a sport but then his life took a dramatic turn. But his wish was to meet me, so we were able to spend the day together. Then he did something I will never forget as long as I live: he gave me the last trophy he had ever won in a race, as well as a picture he had drawn of himself racing, and he even autographed a sheet of paper for me when I asked. How does that not affect you? How does that not change you? Here was a kid (a really cool, fun kid, I should add) who could no longer do what he loved to do because of this life-altering condition, and yet he was still in great spirits and was encouraging to *me* rather than me being the one to lift him up a little bit. Just the fact that he would give me the gift of his last trophy was so special to me and made me want to do even more for the kids in Make-A-Wish.

I always find myself thinking about how unbelievably unfair it is that these wish kids are having to deal with whatever it is that they're facing, but most of them don't seem to see it that way at all. They're just happy to have their wishes granted and to have a good time. You can see in the parents' eyes, of course, the weight of everything they've had to watch their child endure and sometimes even the pain of knowing that the worst is still to come. I've had a few wishes where the children were not expected to recover, and I would just ache for the families. The children are inevitably cheerful and excited, though. It's the parents whom you see struggling between being fully invested in the moment of enjoying themselves and knowing that this probably is one of the last family outings they will ever enjoy together. I remember one mother in California alternating between laughing and crying as she thanked me for the experience my team had given her family. I tried to explain that the honor was all ours—that we had been entrusted with bringing happiness to her son during the most difficult thing he would ever have to face—but there are some situations where words just aren't adequate.

My own children, twins Kadin and Elise, were born six weeks premature and had to spend thirty days in the hospital after they were born before my wife and I were able to bring them home. Just that month was an excruciatingly long time, and I know it was only a very small taste of what these wish families have experienced. For so many of them, the journey is much more difficult, the hospital stays much longer, and the outcome not always a happy one. I know how much pain my wife and I were in as we worried about our own children; I can't imagine the anguish that other families have to endure as the uncertainty drags on or the unthinkable news comes. If I can offer anything—even just one day of encouragement and escape for them—I want to do it.

I have a large photo hanging in the workshop at my farm of a little guy who came out to watch me when he was about five years old and battling cancer. The Ricky Carmichael jersey he is wearing is down to his ankles and the hat is huge on his little head, bald and shiny from the chemotherapy, but he is grinning from ear to ear. It always makes me choke up when I see it because he's not with us anymore, and it seems so wrong to me that such a tiny child should have had such a short life punctuated by so much physical pain. I'm not a very emotional guy, and it takes a lot to make me shed a tear. But I get a pretty big lump in my throat whenever I'm around "my" wish kids. And that photo? I keep it hanging in a prominent place on purpose to always remind me to keep my focus on what matters most.

LIVE IN THE MOMENT

Misty May-Treanor

So much of my life has been spent fixing my eyes on what lays ahead.

I have spent years training for the Olympics, focusing on the competition that

I knew was coming and dedicating all my time and energy preparing.

Then, a few years ago, my mother passed away from cancer. As difficult as it was to see her health deteriorate, that time we had to make memories together and say good-bye was one of the most precious experiences of my life. Little did I know that those experiences were preparing me with the perspective and empathy that would be so important as I began my work with Make-A-Wish. In return, however, Make-A-Wish prepared me for a whole new outlook on the future and how I approach the opportunity to give back.

I'd seen plenty of Make-A-Wish commercials on TV over the years featuring athlete visits or vacations for the family. I'd watch those ads and just grin, thinking, "How cool for that kid to get to go to a theme park with Joe Montana!" or whatever the case may be. You could always see the genuine joy and excitement on the kids' faces, and I knew that I wanted to be a part of bringing that kind of happiness to kids—but I figured that it would be through much smaller ways. As a professional athlete I feel like I have a responsibility to reach out, but I always figured that would mean contacting various organizations to see if they could use volunteers. After all, there are a lot of athletes who fit the "famous" bill a lot better than I do, so I just assumed that I would be the one making first contact. So when Make-A-Wish contacted me and said that there was a young woman whose wish was to meet me, I felt like my own wish was being granted. I kept thinking, "Is this real? Am I really going to get to meet a Make-A-Wish child? That's incredible!" I have zero doubt that I was every bit as excited about hanging out with this girl as she was to hang out with me.

Alissa, a high school sophomore and volleyball player, had been diagnosed with a serious blood-clotting disorder, resulting in large clots throughout her brain, neck, lungs, arms, and hip, and she had had to put her athletic dreams on hold. At the time of our meeting, she was scheduled to soon have a large portion of her left lung removed. We were going to have the chance to meet and talk for a bit while she and her mother spent the day at a theme park in California; it turned out we kind of had different expectations about the day, however. Alissa assumed that she would tour the park for a little bit and then we'd have a little meet and greet. Then I'd leave and she and her mom would go back to enjoying the park. I, on the other hand, figured we were going to spend the whole day together. (Then again, maybe that was just what I wanted to happen, so that was how I proceeded.) So once we met up and visited for a while, I gave her one of my uniforms from a tournament and a signed volleyball, and we talked a bit about her goals and how my career had grown from high school to college and on. And then I suggested we go on a couple of rides . . . and then a couple more . . . and a couple more. We had an absolute blast doing the whole park together. I figured that if she was feeling poorly, she'd say something. She's an athlete, and athletes are obviously pretty tough. I figured that the last thing she wanted was to be treated gingerly or coddled like she was fragile.

Sure enough, we wore each other out that day with all the rides and shows. I was having the time of my life, laughing and talking with Alissa and her mom like they were some of my oldest friends. Alissa was a little shy at first; I'm sure that there is a little stress for some kids, who might think, "All this is for me—I don't want to screw it up!" But her mom and I talked the most at first to kind of get Alissa to feel at ease. Then I started asking her questions about her outfit (it was obvious she was a really fashionable girl) and how she put it together, how she chose her shoes, and so forth, and I think that just broke the ice so that she realized we could just talk about normal stuff. We talked about the challenges of dealing with teenage boys. I asked if she had any pets and what their names were. She wasn't restricted to asking me volleyball questions or worrying that she had to say something meaningful and deep for me to want to stick around. Alissa was there to have the time of her life, and I was just an accessory to that, so I wanted to make sure that she knew that it was a day all about just enjoying herself and leaving all the worries of real life outside the park gates.

I hadn't been to this theme park since I was about ten years old, so she and I were like a couple of kids living it up. She probably thought I was crazy, but I was genuinely enjoying our time together and just acting the way I would around my family. I invited Alissa and her mother to come watch a practice the next day so I could introduce her to my teammate, but their travel plans were such that they couldn't. I teased her: I'd granted her wish, but she couldn't grant mine? That's rough! At the end of the day, I took out my medals and let her take a good look at them; she took a picture wearing them and then we said good-bye. Later that night I sent her a text message thanking her and her mom again for such a great day, not only because I had genuinely enjoyed my time with Alissa, but because it had gotten me thinking.

I was starting to realize that the painful experience of my mother's passing and my wonderful day with Alissa were all pointing to the same lesson for me: live in the moment. Whether it was trying to help a seriously ill teenage girl forget all of her cares or the challenges facing her ahead, or if it was making a few last memories with my mother knowing full well that she would be gone in just a few weeks, I was beginning to understand the importance of focusing on the here and now. Goal setting is very important, and the discipline it taught me has earned me much more than Olympic medals, but it is equally as important to not miss life by focusing too intently on what is ahead. Why bring the grief or pain that you know lies ahead into

the present? Why allow that worry to corrupt the wonderful day you're having right now? Why obsess about what you can't control so that you miss out on the great memories you can make with the things you can control?

The more I thought about that, the more I realized what a gift that lesson really was. It changed my perspective on everything—especially my approach to giving back. Now I really make a point of trying to do more than just talk about my experiences in the Olympics. I bring my medals along whenever it's practical. I let people hold them, wear them, turn them over, and take photos and ask questions and really feel like they are a part of those medals, too. The medals need some polishing sometimes and have gotten a few dents and scratches along the way. But that just means that they've been out there bringing excitement and joy to people instead of being locked away behind glass or in a vault to keep fingerprints, smudges, or nicks from getting on them.

That's the way that life should be, too. We might be a little worse for the wear in the evening, but any little bruises or aches just remind us that we did something, we were active, we *lived*. Spending that day with Alissa, seeing her excitement and courage about charging onto a roller coaster despite having a painful physical condition, showed me how we should all approach each day. I know her looming surgery had to be rattling around in the back of her mind, but she didn't let it bring her down.

We're still in close contact. She keeps me up-to-date on her life; I invite her to share the trivial stuff as well as the important things because, after all, it's the little stuff that makes up most of our day-to-day lives. I love to see that the positive spirit she had before her surgery has continued to be a part of her personality afterward. Even though she has had to sacrifice a lot because of her condition, she still refuses to ever entertain a "Why me?" mentality.

Alissa is now a premed student and Spanish major in college. She says she still can't believe that I spent the entire day with her and then invited her to come watch a practice and pass the volleyball around the next morning.

"A lot of my friends in high school that I played volleyball with were really jealous," she says, laughing. "I have pictures around my apartment of us and people are like, 'Oh my gosh—I can't believe you actually met her!'"

Alissa has had to give up volleyball because of her condition, but she has remained active, running 5Ks and continuing to work out at the gym. Having had as much of her lung removed as she did, doctors did not expect her to be able to engage in much athletic activity at all, but Alissa insists, "I just push really hard because I'm stubborn and I want to prove them wrong."

All lives are tied to each other and we share a responsibility to look out for and encourage one another. If it means jumping in the car to drive up to a school event to show kids positive role models, I'll do it. If it means buying a plane ticket to race out to a hospital room where a terminally ill patient needs a little encouragement, count me in. And I'll probably bring my medals along, too. Each night, I want to be able to look back over the last twenty-four hours and know that I really invested myself in that day, pouring everything I had into making the most of that time and making the world a little bit better in whatever tiny way I could contribute. There's no better feeling than that.

All lives are tied to each other and we share a responsibility to look out for and encourage one another.

WE CAN ALL DO SOMETHING

Barry Sanders

When you are a professional athlete, you have certain

responsibilities. It's just that simple. And one of those responsibilities

is to make sure that you are reaching out to the fans who need you most—

the ones who aren't just watching your games for fun but who

cheer for you because when they are watching you on the

field, they don't have to worry about their illnesses.

But here's the thing: when you are a professional athlete, you are afforded a lot of privileges. And one of those privileges is getting to spend time with those same kids—the ones who turn to your games as an escape from their painful treatments or the sickness brought on by chemotherapy.

It's really humbling when you learn that a child who could wish for anything at all picked *you*. That makes it a pretty serious task to make sure that you give your all to that meeting so the child has no regrets about his or her choice. When I was still playing, I usually tried to do my wishes during Saturday practices. The child and his or her family got to tour the stadium and watch us go through our final pregame prep

for Sunday's game. That not only gave the child a behind-the-scenes look at what we did, but it also meant that I was able to dedicate as much time afterward as the child wanted without having to be distracted by the clock counting down to kickoff. It was all very relaxed. Sometimes the kids come in a little starstruck, but they quickly realize that once all the layers are stripped away, we're all just people—even the folks on TV—and there is a human side to our lives, too, that we are eager to share with them. We would take some photos, sign some autographs, share some laughs, and talk about whatever they wanted to talk about. I liked to ask them about their interests and hobbies so that I could get to know them a little better, but I made sure they had plenty of time to ask me any questions they might have, too. The most common one I got is one I didn't know how to answer, though: "How did you get so fast?" Some kids wanted to know what it's like to play in the NFL, but not just because they were curious fans. Several kids I've met were athletes before their diagnoses and still had hopes and dreams to compete in sports someday, whether their dreams went as far as the pros or they simply wanted to be able to run after a ball again.

I realize that I just wrote about the wishes in the past tense, and it's true that I certainly don't get called as often now since I retired in 1999. But every now and then, I am surprised by a request. For example, in 2008, a ten-year-old boy named Brandon made a wish to meet me. Even though he was only a year old when I announced my retirement, everyone in his family is a Detroit Lions fan, so he grew up not only watching the current team's games, but also playing all of his dad's old videos of past seasons, and he became one of my biggest fans. When Brandon was diagnosed with Burkitt's lymphoma, he made a wish—and he knew right away that he wanted it to involve the current Detroit Lions team and me. In early November of that year, Brandon and his family were invited to attend practice to meet the players. He got to play catch on the field and get a number of autographs from the guys. But what made his wish especially cool was that it was the ten thousandth wish stemming from a Make-A-Wish national corporate sponsorship, and for the 2008 Thanksgiving Day parade in Detroit three weeks later, Brandon got to be part of the corporate sponsor's float. That afternoon, he and his family attended the Lions' annual Thanksgiving Day football game and, at halftime, were brought into a private suite to hang out with my two children and me. I don't know who enjoyed the experience more: Brandon or me. I think we all really had a great time. He was such a neat kid, and his family was so supportive of everything he was going through and grateful for the experiences he was able to have as part of his wish. For my part, I loved getting to meet a young person who was such a student of the game, an incredibly enthusiastic fan, and so

amazingly brave. (And, of course, it doesn't hurt to get to talk to someone who is still excited about some of my own past football games!) Even though his cancer was very aggressive, he was also determined to not let it define him.

The thing that gets me the most about kids like Brandon and all of "my" wish kids, I think, is the fact that most of them really do understand how serious their situations are. They aren't naïve. They know that the odds are often stacked against them, and while they are hopeful about the future, they also often know that they may not have many days left. And yet, they are all happy kids determined to make each day count. That never ceases to amaze me and leaves a lasting impact. They are going through so much more than I will ever go through, and yet they choose to dwell on the positive. What a tremendous life lesson for all of us! Make-A-Wish experiences deliver a certain kind of reality to

your doorstep; it makes you come face-to-face with the sort of thing that's too easy to think: "It could never happen to me." The fact is, diseases don't discriminate. These illnesses could strike anyone.

I grew up in a big family, surrounded by brothers, sisters, and cousins, and now I have children of my own, so I can't imagine not being around kids. Whenever you say good-bye to a wish child, though, there is always a bit of sadness mixed with pride. You are sad because you know what childhood should be like— happy, carefree, full of hope—but you know that these sick kids have to shoulder a much heavier load. But at the same time, there is such a sense of pride in how they stand up under the pressures and unimaginable stress. You can't help but feel inspired by each and every wish child you meet, as well as the families that support them.

Make-A-Wish is such a tremendous way to honor kids who are making the best of the cards they've been dealt, and I am so humbled to have been a part of their work. And by reading this book, you are helping to show your support as well. But you can do even more than that. I urge you to seriously consider giving your time and talents to make a child's wish come true. My particular skill set allowed me to offer some kids a wonderful escape from their difficult times. What about you? What is unique about you that you can offer? Some children have wishes about art or dance or superheroes or building things or anything else you can imagine. I have no doubt that there is something about you that Make-A-Wish can use to help a seriously ill child's wish come true. Together, we can help make a difference in the lives of some of the most precious and deserving people in our communities. Thank you for caring.

DEFYING EXPECTATIONS

Anthony Robles

In the summer of 2012, Dylan came home from wrestling camp complaining of intense pain in the back of his legs. The pain only increased as he began football practice, and repeated visits to various doctors resulted in diagnoses ranging from pulled hamstrings to deteriorating muscles.

Finally, when the pain became so severe that the teenager could hardly walk, an emergency room visit resulted in an MRI that revealed three tumors on his spine. Dylan was airlifted to a children's hospital in Indianapolis for a biopsy, which came back positive for cancer. He had surgery to remove the largest tumor, and thirty-three proton radiation treatments to eliminate the smaller tumors.

The previous season, Dylan's wrestling coach had showed his team films of various college wrestlers to study their technique. Apparently I captured his attention—me, Anthony Robles from Arizona State, who was born with only one leg. Months later, as Dylan was recovering from his treatments, he caught one of my TV interviews about my book, *Unstoppable: From Underdog to Undefeated.* "He said, 'Mom, I need his book. I've got to have his book,'" Dylan's mother, Kay, recalled.

She drove to South Bend to buy it the week it was released, and Dylan immediately sat down to pore over it. He was a boy who always found reading a bit challenging and definitely boring, so Kay was amazed at the way the book affected her son. "He came out of his room when he had finished reading it and asked, 'If he can wrestle with one leg, why can't I wrestle with cancer?'"

Kay knew that her son had felt a profound connection with my story, so she sent me an e-mail at the best address she could find to thank me for what I had done to inspire her child. I wrote back and asked if I could call Dylan. Dylan and I spoke for about five or ten minutes, and I told Dylan, "Keep your head up. We're brothers in wrestling." That same night, Dylan came down with a 103-degree fever, probably as a result of an infection from his radiation treatment, and had to be readmitted to the hospital. But his mother said he had a huge grin the whole time. Then, when Dylan learned he was eligible for a wish, he said he wanted to meet me. I wanted to meet him, too.

If you asked most people to describe the physical condition of a high school or college wrestler, they would probably say things like "strong" and "quick on his feet." They probably would not say, "missing a limb" or "fighting spinal tumors." But that's exactly what brought me and Dylan together.

Let me introduce myself. I'm a three-time all-American wrestler from Arizona State University, NCAA titleholder, and member of the National Wrestling Hall of Fame. What makes my career unique is that I was born without my right leg. I started wrestling in high school, and even though I started out as an easy win for anyone matched against me, I soon developed my own style and went undefeated in the 125-and-under weight class my last two years of high school, winning the national high school championships my senior year. I walked on to the wrestling team at ASU and went on to enjoy success in my college career, too. Now I provide commentary for a sports network, I'm an athlete, and I am a motivational speaker—which is how I ended up on the other end of a wish request for Dylan.

At sixteen years of age, Dylan was a high school wrestler who was served a devastating diagnosis of myxopapillary ependymoma. MEPN, as it is commonly called, occurs when the supportive tissue of the brain causes a slow-growing tumor to arise on the spine. But even as he was undergoing his treatments, his doctors were continually amazed at his energy and determination to wrestle again just as soon as his doctors gave him the all clear. Dylan felt as if people had low expectations for him because of his illness. One of the main things driving him was to prove that he was not listening to the naysayers.

When the request came in to me, it was extremely humbling. My manager explained it to me, and I was a little shocked. I'd known about Make-A-Wish because of their occasional partnership with college athletics for various events, but I never imagined that I would be involved with actually making a child's wish come true. Let's be honest: How many competitive wrestlers (not professional wrestlers, who are very different types of athletes) can most people name off the tops of their heads? We're not exactly a headline-stealing sport. I wasn't sure what Dylan was hoping for, or even how his attitude would be about his illness. I just knew that he could have wished for anything, but he chose to meet me. Talk about feeling nervous!

The foundation made arrangements for us to meet when I was speaking at an event in Des Moines, Iowa. Dylan and his family live in Indiana, so they flew in to hear my speech. It was only Dylan's second time flying; the first time was when he had been airlifted to the children's hospital.

About two hours before the banquet began, we met at the hotel: Dylan, his parents, his three little sisters, and me. The first thing that struck me about Dylan was his smile. He had the biggest grin on his face. It was amazing to see this young man who was going through so much—not just with his cancer and treatments but also being kept from doing the sport he loved—be all smiles. We were all in evening clothes for the event, and I made a joke about the fact that the planner must not have known what they were doing, allowing two wrestlers to crash their classy banquet. Dylan laughed, and then we just started talking like old friends about everything from wrestling to girlfriends to the fact that I'd just bought a house. It was just a casual, relaxed conversation between two real people, connecting over real life.

It was great, too, to be able to compare notes about the wrestlers we both knew. Dylan had attended the Big Ten wrestling championships in the past and gotten the autographs of some of those same guys I had wrestled against. What I found was that we had so, so much in common. He and I were both motivated by the fact that people might dismiss us on the surface. While that might be discouraging for some people, it was a huge motivation for Dylan and for me. We also shared a very matter-of-fact outlook on our health situations: I was blessed. He was blessed. We didn't know why we had to go through difficult circumstances that seemed so different from what many of our peers were dealing with, but that was simply the hand we'd been dealt. Now what were we going to do with it?

It was so encouraging to me to meet a teenager who already had such a mature attitude toward things. And the more I considered our time together, the more I realized that those lessons are true for all of us, whether our challenges take a physical form, like mine and Dylan's, or whether they appear in a different way. The fact is, we will all have difficult times; we'll all have challenges thrown at us. But it is up to us to decide if we are going to let those bad times win, or if we are going to use them to make us stronger. Dylan is such a clear example of someone who was determined to take the second option.

He told me about how his community had pitched in to cheer him on during his fight and to help support his whole family while he was undergoing surgery, proton radiation therapy, and other treatments. There were fundraisers and even a prayer vigil at a local baseball park attended by about three hundred people. Knowing his love for wrestling, some of his aunts and uncles even made T-shirts with the slogan "Take down cancer" playing off of the term *takedown*, meaning when a wrestler is brought to the mat and controlled by the body of his opponent. The shirts were sold so that people could show their concern for Dylan while also supporting his family. Clearly, he had a great team cheering him on, in addition to an incredible, loving family to walk beside him. Even so, it had been a tough journey, and there was still a long road ahead of him. But Dylan? Dylan was just waiting for the okay from the doctors to start wrestling again.

We talked about our goals, and I told him how I still carry a sticky note in my wallet that I wrote when I was about his age, when I had first started wrestling. It says, "State Champion." At the time, no one would have possibly believed I'd ever have a winning record, let alone achieve a state championship; but I believed and I was committed to it, and I believe that was what made the difference. I wanted Dylan to see that and hopefully feel encouraged to set his own goals for what he would accomplish despite his challenges. But he was already way ahead of me. Mark my words: you are going to hear great things about that young man in the future. He has his head in the right place, and his heart is absolutely enormous!

We've stayed in touch, and I've been able to introduce Dylan to some of my college wrestling buddies, which is cool, since in our sport college is kind of like our pros. But one of the best parts of the experience for me has been the staying power of Dylan's story in my life. I've found myself thinking about him and his incredible outlook over and over again. He is such an inspiration for me because he has reminded me that no matter what you go through, someone else has it harder. In Dylan's case, he's had to battle unspeakable pain as the tumors affected the nerves in his spine; that is something I never had to deal with. I may be missing a leg, but I never had to deal with any physical pain from it.

Tough times are inevitable, but we are each faced with three choices: we can walk through, we can crawl through, or we can give up. Sometimes, we may not have the strength to walk through the way we'd like to, but as long as we keep moving forward, dragging ourselves toward the other end of that tunnel, we are making progress and keeping hope alive. Dylan is an incredible example of a young man who is not focused on his disease—not on his pain, not on his treatments, and not on everything he is missing out on. He has his sights set far beyond all of that to the day when he not only can return to the mat as a wrestler but can stand up in the middle as a champion—not just of the match, but of life.

FINDING A CAUSE

Tim Hudson

In the winter of 1999, I was sure I was living the dream.

I had been called up to the majors in June, and now, after pitching half a

season for the Oakland A's, I felt like I was really finding my rhythm.

I'd recently gotten married to the girl of my dreams, Kim, and we'd just flown back to California from Birmingham, Alabama. That particular afternoon, I had just wrapped up being part of the A's Caravan, in which a number of Oakland players travel around to various cities in California visiting local elementary schools, doing radio shows, and making public relations appearances. There were about eight or ten of us driving back to Oakland together.

Kim and I had been talking in the car about possible organizations we'd like to partner with, since that had always been a goal we'd shared. When I made it in the majors, we were going to make sure that we really invested ourselves in a charity or foundation of some kind. We both come from pretty humble backgrounds, so we wanted to make sure that we were giving back from the blessings we'd been given. There were a number of really great groups out there doing some important work, but the problem was that we hadn't found one that seemed to really speak to us yet.

Our discussion was put on hold when the A's Caravan pulled into a restaurant in Redding, California, for dinner. Because of the size of our party, the hostess escorted us upstairs to a room designated for larger groups in need of a little more privacy. We found ourselves sharing the room with a group of six or eight kids who, it turned out, were all part of Make-A-Wish . . . and my life was never the same.

I'd heard of Make-A-Wish, of course. For more than thirty years, they have been taking care of kids all over the country. But I'd never really given them much serious thought until recently, when Oakland was playing Seattle on the road. There was a child there with his family, enjoying his wish to spend the day at a Mariners game. I remember seeing the players going over to talk with him and the huge grin on his face whenever they did. It was clear he was having the time of his life, making a special memory with his family that had nothing to do with hospital rooms or medical treatments. But at that point, my focus was just on staying in the big leagues; there was a part of me that worried I might not be able to make a career of it after all. So I didn't really give a whole lot of thought to Make-A-Wish after that . . . until the A's public relations coordinator who was traveling with us went over to the other table, chatted briefly with the adults, and then reported back to us: "Those kids over there are all part of the Make-A-Wish program. Why don't you guys go over and say hello?"

We were already in outreach mode from our day of visits, interviews, and meet and greets, which I think helped the conversation flow a little easier. Baseball players aren't always naturally talkative folks, and it's even harder to know what to say when you realize that you're looking at a child with a life-threatening illness—a kid twenty years your junior who has already faced far tougher obstacles than anything in your own life. It's incredibly humbling.

Just watching those kids at the restaurant—some of them obviously suffering from some pretty severe conditions—run around and laugh and simply relish life made me embarrassed for the little things I sometimes let ruin my entire day. Here were kids who had all the odds stacked against them, and yet they had such positive attitudes. It made me realize how incredibly blessed I really was to have enjoyed the health and opportunities I'd been given.

When we got into the car after dinner, Kim and I just looked at each other and smiled. There was no need for discussion or questions; we both knew that we had been put at that very restaurant at that very time for a reason. We had discovered our foundation, and just like that, we knew we had found a cause for which we were passionate.

And so our partnership with Make-A-Wish began. We organized a golf tournament at a country club in Pleasant Hill, California, to benefit the Make-A-Wish Greater Bay Area chapter, with all proceeds going to help grant wishes. Until we got involved, I had no idea that it can cost around $7,000 to send a family to a theme park for a week, when health concerns and accommodations are taken into account along with travel, lodging, meals, and other expenses. I remember being so touched that first night when I met a little girl from the Sacramento area named Miranda who had brain cancer. She was the sweetest child, and very ill. She had initially wished for her family to go to a theme park but then decided that was "too much to ask for" and just requested a Sacramento Kings game instead since she already lived in town. I knew the foundation was going to do whatever it could to make her original wish come true, but I didn't want any other child to ever feel that it was "too much" to wish for a trip like that for their family to make special memories together. I wanted to make sure that I was doing everything in my power to give Make-A-Wish all the tools it needed.

That first golf tournament left me sweating. It costs quite a lot to put one on that runs smoothly and attracts interest from potential donors, and I was terrified that everything might go bust. When the numbers came in from registration, we just broke even from the golfers' entry fees; there was a silent auction following the dinner with a number of items donated by my teammates and some local businesses. I found myself just praying that we would bring in just a little bit more—just enough to make all the time and effort worth it for the foundation. There were several Make-A-Wish kids there with their families, and I wanted them to feel like this whole event really meant something and that people really cared about them.

Some of my teammates from the A's had shown up to offer their support—guys like Jason Giambi, Mark Mulder, Barry Zito, Eric Chavez, Ramon Hernandez, Frank Menechino, Aaron Harang, Jim Mecir, Scott Hatteberg, and Jason Isringhausen. In fact, more than half the team showed up on an off day just to be a part of it. It was pretty amazing, but I was still nervous about whether we would be able to make it all really count for Make-A-Wish. When I saw that the first item up for auction was a jersey I had signed, my heart sank. I guess they thought it was a nice way to pay tribute to me, but I was still a new player, and I wanted to see the bidding start on a much more exciting item that would bring in more money. But when it was over, my jersey had gone for more than $10,000. I couldn't believe it. Why on earth would some-one pay that much for something signed by me? But then, the winner (who happened to be one of my teammates) did something even more amazing: he turned to the wish child sitting closest to him and handed over the jersey with a big smile. The next item up was a jersey signed by Giambi, and I can assure you that it went for considerably more than mine had. The winner of that jersey then gave it to another wish child. The place went wild. For the rest of the night, bidders were outdoing one another until every kid there had something. Barry Zito even stood up to model his jersey, which elicited quite a few whistles and cheers from the rest of us. I quickly lost count of where we were, but nothing could have prepared me for the final numbers: more than $100,000 had been raised just on that one night.

I was so tremendously humbled by the incredible generosity of the golfers who participated, not to mention my teammates and others who had donated items for the auction and participated in the bidding. Seeing that level of compassion and enthusiasm for those children and their families was incredibly moving and made me want to support the foundation even more.

When I was traded to the Atlanta Braves in 2005, Kim and I both knew that our dedication to Make-A-Wish would move to Atlanta with us. Since then, we have been incredibly blessed to be named ambassadors for the foundation, helping to grant wishes in a variety of ways and speaking publicly about the wonderful work that they do. I've been a part of dozens of wishes for children who want to visit the stadium and meet the Braves, and I am so blessed to have an incredible group of teammates who are every bit as excited as I am about meeting those children and making the day special. It's as if the amazing spirit of those children, their parents, and their siblings rubs off on us and puts every minor inconvenience or annoyance in our own lives in perspective. I think we get as much out of each experience as the wish kids do because of the respect and trust we develop for one another as a team when we see each other going the extra mile to reach out to our special guests.

I'm also blessed to have a wife who has such a heart for helping others. In fact, Kim serves with me as an honorary co-chair of the Celebration of Wishes gala, an event in the Atlanta area every fall that serves as a major avenue for raising funds and awareness of the foundation's work in Georgia. Additionally, we partner with

Make-A-Wish to throw a holiday party each year in which both the sick children and their siblings receive a gift card. This is one of my favorite outreach efforts because it includes the brothers and sisters in the celebration. Often, the other siblings can feel overshadowed by all of the time, attention, and resources that are, necessarily, dedicated to the child who is ill. This can be especially difficult for younger children to understand. By including all of the children, it helps to reinforce that every member of the family matters, that their strength and courage are important, and that their experience matters, too.

As my own three children get older, I am genuinely excited for them to be able to become involved, getting to know some of the children with whom the foundation works and really understanding why it matters so much to Kim and me. I hope that they grow up to appreciate the courage and strength of these families and that they learn from the incredible examples of hope and tenacity.

It is clearer than ever to me now why I ended up at that restaurant in Redding, California, back in 1999. At a moment when it seemed that my every wish was coming true, it was time for me to begin using the tremendous blessings and opportunities I'd been given to help grant the wishes of others. I will forever be grateful to the special children I met that night and for the indelible mark their spirits and stories have left on my life and my heart.

IT'S ALL ABOUT HOPE

Tony Hawk

The look on the kid's face was priceless.

"Hey—is your mom here?" I asked, stepping into his hospital room like

it was the most natural thing in the world for me to be there.

There were several seconds of shocked silence as he tried to form words but couldn't seem to make a sound. Finally, he managed to reply, "No. She had to step out for a minute . . . but she won't believe this. I—I have to call her."

I couldn't help but laugh. I knew the visit was a surprise (I'd arranged the whole thing with his parents ahead of time), but the reaction was more shocked and amazed than I could have hoped for. We ended up spending a great afternoon together. I brought him some DVDs, one of my video games, and a skateboard. We sat and talked as he underwent his treatment, and it was really a good time. I had one of my best friends with me, too—Kevin Staab, who is also a professional skateboarder—so it was almost like we had a twofer wish for a kid who loved skateboarding.

It's still amazing to me whenever I find out that someone has requested to meet me for their wish, because I can't imagine being a kid with the opportunity to wish for anything . . . and wanting to meet a *skateboarder*. I guess when I was a little kid, skateboarding just wasn't a "thing" yet, so it's not like I ever had anyone doing the sport who was famous or whom I looked up to. I guess it's still a little shocking to me that the skateboarding world has grown to become all it has. In fact, the very first wish I granted was back when I was seventeen or eighteen years old—pretty much still a kid myself—and back then, too, it seemed weird to me that someone would make that request, because skateboarding definitely wasn't anything in the mainstream yet; it was still kind of an underground, countercultural activity. So that any sick child would care about skating enough to want to meet someone involved with it and actually know who I was and what I did was incredibly humbling to me. That feeling of humility toward what the Make-A-Wish organization does has stayed with me ever since. Because of that, I feel like I want to give the kids so much more than just a visit with me. Now, I like to think that I'm fun to hang out with, but I feel like any child who is keeping his or her chin up through hospital stays and painful medical treatments and procedures deserves something a whole lot better than a day with Tony Hawk. I like to do whatever I can to give them as big an experience as possible with their wish. It doesn't always work out this way, but if I'm able to swing it with my travel schedule, I try to make arrangements to meet the kids right at their home or in the hospital. "Save your wish to go to someplace fun," I like to joke with them. Lots of kids still come out to see me in Southern California, though, which is where I have all my ramps. In fact, I've done close to fifty wishes out there, and it never gets old.

I find that no matter where the visit takes place, it always renews my sense of hope in the human spirit. The kids are usually kind of shy at first, and the parents are surprised, saying, "He usually talks nonstop!" But I get it. It's kind of overwhelming to have that guy you know from TV or video games or skateboarding magazines sitting next to you. I've done this enough times to know that it won't take long for the ice to break. Once the kids warm up and start feeling more comfortable, the first question is almost always about whether I ever get to hang out with other famous skaters. "Do you know Bam Margera? Ryan Sheckler? Paul Rodriguez?" It just cracks me up. It's so clear that they are looking for insight into a world they've always wondered about, and it's really cool to see how excited they are to finally get to talk to someone who knows about it. I've had many kids replay my career highlights to me: "Do you remember the time that you nailed that one trick?" Yes, I remember that. Other times, they are eager to ask about my worst moments: "Do you remember the time you fell and broke your toe?" Yes, I remember that, too. I just love how they want to somehow validate all the things they've seen or heard about my career as if to verify that it's real, that I'm real, that the falls and the tricks and the big moments and big crashes are all real.

I often joke that due to the ages of my own kids—nineteen, thirteen, seven, and four—I have my own built-in focus groups. I know what kids in each age group are into and what sorts of things they enjoy. This helps me tremendously in relating with the wish kids and knowing how to answer the questions they want to ask me about my career or skateboarding in general. In that way, the wish kids are just like every other kid their age: curious, excited, and eager to learn more about something they love. But the kids also have a tremendous strength about them. It's so incredible to see how these kids have learned to find happiness in other things, despite their normal lives being taken away from them. That's a very powerful lesson for all of us, I think. No matter what situation you are facing, there is room for joy and room for hope.

If we're at my office, where my ramps are all located, I always ask the kids if they'd like to try riding some boards. Some of them say that they'd rather just watch. But others are excited to give boardwork a try. Usually, they are okay with just doing some basic things, though every now and then there is a kid who wants to try some really wild tricks that would probably endanger us both. I have to explain that when I skate holding a camera, I can fall and let the camera take the brunt of the impact, so I can do much more extreme stuff. But when I'm skating with a child, it's a lot more difficult to fall in such a way that protects them, so we have to be a little tamer. There was one little boy just a few months ago who had lost a leg to a disease and had traveled out to see me. I asked if he wanted to get on a board and his eyes absolutely lit up. So he balanced himself, and I started pushing him up and down the ramps. I was afraid we weren't doing anything he would find too exciting, so I asked if he was doing okay. "Yeah!" he almost shouted. "This is the most fun I've had since I found out I was sick!"

It's moments like those when I remind myself to just stay focused on the kids and to make the day all about them and not about how their big smiles and cheerful personalities are blowing my mind. The parents are usually off to the side, getting incredibly emotional during all of this, but I try to make sure that I keep myself together so the kids get my full attention instead of wondering why Tony Hawk is getting choked up. My friend Kevin accompanies me on a lot of wishes, and he will freely admit that he is usually an emotional wreck during them. More than once I've turned to him and whispered, "You gonna make it?" because he is so overwhelmed by the amazing experience that we're having, even as the wish kid is having an awesome experience of his or her own.

And I usually get something out of it, too, though not always just an emotional boost. Several years ago, one boy was watching me skate and asked if I would do a "rodeo flip." Now, normally when the kids make requests to see certain tricks, it's stuff I can make happen for them. Occasionally, they want to see some kind of crazy combination that is possible on the video game but not really in real life—at least not by me. But when that boy asked to see a rodeo flip, my heart sank a little. The trick is an inverted 540-degree move that basically looks as if the skater is doing a backflip. I used to do it pretty often, but then it just gradually got worked out of my regular rotation. Now, here I was supposed to be granting the wish of a sick child, and his wish was to see me do a trick I hadn't done in probably close to a decade. What choice did I have? I took a deep breath and gave it a try . . . and managed to nail it. I don't know who was more excited—him or me. I mean, thanks to that one wish kid, I relearned a trick in one day and ended up running that trick for a year or two afterward. (Then I took a hard fall on it and ended up dropping it from my rotation again. But still, it was cool!)

I love that my own kids are often able to be there during wishes, as well. It's so awesome to be able to see them interact with those children and see the maturity and strength that they carry; I think it helps my children have a whole new perspective on what really matters. So your phone is acting up and you can't play a mobile game right now; in the big scheme of things, how much does that really matter—especially when you've just met a child your age who is going through a life-altering ordeal? The wish children always seem to radiate such hope and joy that they can't help but affect everyone around them.

That's one of the reasons that my work with Make-A-Wish has been so meaningful. There are a lot of great organizations and charities out there, but they aren't all able to offer such empirical, tangible results. One of the reasons I love Make-A-Wish is that I get to be present for the fruit of my contribution. I get to actually be a part of the big day. They aren't asking for anything more than my presence, and I love that because I get to really see the direct impact of their work.

When a wish motivates a child with his or her treatments, or helps to encourage the entire family, that's about so much more than just the few hours that we spent together. That's about showing the child, parents, and siblings that people care. They care a lot. The fact that these kids are still out there every day, fighting whatever disease or condition they're facing despite a sometimes very uncertain future, should inspire the rest of us to tackle head-on whatever challenge we've been dealt, because that's really the only way to live. Make-A-Wish isn't just about giving a special day to a seriously ill child; it's about restoring hope. For all of us.

"This is the most fun
I've had since I found out
I was sick!"

GRANTING WISHES
MAKES ME BETTER

Landon Donovan

Going into a game in Salt Lake City, the L.A. Galaxy was at a low point

in our season as a soccer team. As the game began, I spotted my young friend

Cody smiling from the front row, the way he always does whenever

we play in Salt Lake, and I felt a little tug of hope that maybe

this game would finally be the one to break the slump.

It didn't start too well, with our opponent scoring twice in a row. But then the Galaxy rallied and did what we do best: we won the game 3–2, and I'm proud to say that two of those goals were mine. It was wonderful to see Cody afterward and to get a big hug from him on the sidelines.

I first met Cody several years ago, when he was still a teenager living in Twin Falls, Idaho. He was an avid soccer player, youth league coach, and MLS fan, so when he was put in contact with Make-A-Wish due to his cancer, he knew immediately what he wanted. I was fortunate enough to be a part of that wish. We bonded instantly and kept in touch via e-mail, texts, and phone calls even after his wish was granted. As he grew up to a young man of twenty, he continued to attend every L.A.

Galaxy game he could when we played in Salt Lake City. He would always come down to the front of the stands so I could give him a hug before warm-ups, and then we'd talk after the game. He always had friends with him, just having a great time where he didn't have to think about the really rough parts of his life and his disease.

Recently, when his cancer came back more aggressively, he even called me to get my opinion on his treatment options. I'm obviously not a medical professional, but he wanted some honest advice, so we talked a while. Finally, I just told him, "You have to trust your gut and do what you think is right, because in the end, the decision has to come from you." He had faced a long, painful battle, and I really admired the fact that he tried to talk to a lot of people to feel confident he was making the best decision.

That's the kind of incredible impact that a wish can have on both "sides"—for the child who asked for the wish and for the people involved in making it come true. You forge relationships. You learn from each other. Your world becomes a little bigger. I know that I've grown a bit with every wish I've granted. When I first started out, I knew the basic concept of Make-A-Wish, but it wasn't until I was directly involved that I really understood what it was all about. I was with the San Jose Earthquakes when I started to get involved with wishes, and now, as I get older, I realize how much more I appreciate the experience. Every wish experience has touched me and changed me for the better in some way so that I really take each one to heart and feel more intensely the power of meeting that child, and then staying a part of his or her life.

All athletes get asked from time to time to do various appearances or outreach events, and many of those things are really for good causes. But the problem is that the list can become so long and so pressing that when you see another event on your calendar, you think, "Okay, that's the next appearance, the next meeting, the next

thing." And you do it because it's on your schedule and you're supposed to meet that commitment, but not because your heart is really in it. It's easy to forget the human element involved. But then you cut to the moment you see a kid's face when they shake your hand for the first time, and that's when it hits you that, out of everything they could possibly want in the world, they asked to meet you. It gives me goose bumps. It's an exciting feeling, but it's also a big responsibility, and the older I have gotten, the more seriously I take it. You're dealing with a life, and this wish day is a big moment in that life.

It's amazing the kind of perspective that meeting with those kids can give you. I live in a world where it's easy to think that the game on Saturday is all there is. But then there is an afternoon where a wish kid attends practice, and Saturday's results are the farthest thing from his or her mind. They're just happy, in many cases, to be outside, away from hospitals or their bed or wherever else they have had to spend most of their time. It suddenly makes Saturday's game results seem a lot less important to me, too, to watch those kids, many of whom are literally fighting for their lives, who are happy to be alive, who are happy to see my team, and who are happy to have an escape from their reality. They are just living in the moment, soaking everything up and having fun. When you take a step back and look at it, it's beautiful—and it's a good reminder that there are some things that are a lot more important than a soccer game.

Usually, a wish child will attend a practice a day or two ahead of time and then get special seats at Saturday's game. With both the U.S. national soccer team and the L.A. Galaxy, we have some really great people who work with Make-A-Wish to coordinate the logistics and who make sure I know right where the family is sitting on game day so I can talk to them afterward. Even though I know that the excitement of the game is probably more interesting to the kids, the practice days are my favorite because they are much more intimate, without all the commotion and crowds. The wish kid will come out with their family and, if they're interested, will do warm-ups with us to whatever degree they're able—running laps, doing drills, dribbling the ball. We've had a lot of kids say, "I wish I was a member of the Galaxy," so we try to do whatever we can to make sure that they feel like a member of the team during warm-ups, including giving them uniforms. Then they are able to sit in the stands and watch our team practice, which is neat because it provides the child with a different perspective than they would normally have.

Those times after practice mean the most to me, though. We often have a lot of media around, but I don't want the child to feel crowded out or uncomfortable because there is a camera in their face or really bright lights shining in their eyes. So I usually end up walking the family away from all the reporters and sports journalists

so that we can spend some time getting to know each other in a more natural and relaxed setting. I try to give them as much time as they want—and not just the child who made the wish, but also the parents and any siblings or cousins or friends they brought along as well.

I don't think the parents of seriously ill children get enough credit. The parents are the ones working on a daily basis to keep their child alive and keep their family's lives in some kind of order. It's nice for them to have a break and a minivacation from all of that, where they can just enjoy seeing their child smiling and happy and enjoying life. I feel for the siblings, too, and I want to make sure that they don't feel forgotten, because sometimes so much attention has been piled on the sick child that the other children feel left out.

Sometimes, the kids are a little tongue-tied at first because they look at you like you're their idol—someone they've watched on TV or followed in sports magazines . . . and now here you are in the flesh! I think that can be a little overwhelming sometimes, but it doesn't take long before they stop seeing you as some kind of mythical figure and start seeing you as just a person and a friend. Our conversations could cover anything, though I generally try to avoid talking about their condition too much unless they want to. I ask how they are feeling and learn enough to be able to follow up with them later in terms of where they are hoping to be with their treatment or recovery. However, I don't want to make them feel like they are their illness or that their identity is completely tied up with their health. We talk about school or hobbies or soccer or whatever interests them. One question a lot of kids ask is, "What kind of car do you drive?" It always makes me laugh that in the middle of all of the excitement of a wish or an upcoming game, that's something that is really pressing on their minds; and when I tell them I drive a regular SUV, they aren't nearly as excited as they were. I think it helps to knock me down from that "idol" pedestal a bit, which is good. But I think it's also an important lesson that because they're human, they can get caught up in materialistic things just like the rest of us. If they understand that I'm just a normal guy and I drive a normal car, I think it helps reinforce that life isn't about status symbols or lavish spending.

You have to be very careful about what you say when talking with kids, though. Kids really do look up to sports figures, and if they like you enough to make meeting you their wish, I think you have a charge to make sure that the things you say and do are not only real and honest but also responsible. I don't ever want someone to make a decision based on advice I offered when I know nothing about the subject or to think that they should do something that I might have mistakenly "endorsed" in our conversation when I really have no clue. Sometimes kids will ask you questions that you aren't sure how to answer, and in those cases I think it's best to be honest and say, "I don't know. But I do care." That's why I think those postpractice conversations are my favorite part of the wish-granting process, because they are so real—just people talking with people. That's where you really make the connections that sustain the relationship long after they've all gone home.

I also try to take the opportunity during practice to introduce the kids to my teammates (there was a certain Mr. David Beckham on my team whom they always were excited to meet), which not only lets them feel even more included in the team, but also gives them more people to cheer for during the game. I absolutely love hearing "my" wish kid shouting for other teammates they met at practice, like Mike Magee or Todd Dunivant, when we play.

I don't know the exact statistic, or if there is any real way to prove this through hard numbers, but I am absolutely convinced that I play better when a Make-A-Wish kid comes. I know it affects me, and I think it affects everyone. There was one game last year when a wish child from Colorado named Brendan came out and was just a really special kid. He was shy at first but eventually started opening up, and we had a great time hanging out and talking. Personally, I was in a bit of a scoring slump—I hadn't scored a goal in ten consecutive games at that point. But the day of the game, with Brendan in the stands, I scored not once, but twice. I'll never forget that. And that's how it is just about every time; I am a better player at the games when the wish kids are there.

I firmly believe that the mental, physical, and emotional are all connected. I know that when I've gotten sick or gotten injured, it was usually during times when I wasn't mentally or emotionally centered the way I would like to be. I definitely see evidence of that balance come into play with how I'm able to perform on the field on days when wishes are granted. It makes a difference for me. It makes me better—not just as a player, but as a person.

The power of feeling emotionally charged makes a difference for the kids, too, I think. So many of them tell me during our visit, "I'm going to stay strong, I'm going to keep fighting, and I'm going to keep battling my illness because I know I can do it." It always amazes and humbles me because I don't always act that way or have such a positive attitude and so much mental toughness. There are days when I think to myself, "It's too tough. I can't do it." But these kids do it. They persevere. And while it's tragically true that not all of them end up winning the fight, they never seem to give up easily or allow the experience to make them bitter or angry. It's incredible to see that, and it's incredible to feel like you were invited along to be part of that journey, part of impacting that amazing life.

The way I see it, if you really want to help someone or change their life, you can't do that in a couple hours and a photograph or two; you impact their lives by staying in touch, staying involved, and genuinely caring. I think the reason I had  such a good relationship with Cody was because he had me as someone outside of his own immediate world whom he still felt like he trusted and could call for advice or just to talk to. That's why I am always so excited when we play in Kansas City and I get to see Tasha and her family, who always say hello during warm-ups and stick around to talk after games. We've stayed in touch long after her wish was over, and the reward is a connection much bigger than it would have been if we had just met for one day and then I never saw her or thought of her again. It's like I have a network of family and friends all over the country made up of the various wish kids I know in the different cities where we play, which makes me feel incredibly lucky.

The connections that Make-A-Wish makes possible allow you to establish a relationship that is life-changing for both you and the child.

I am especially reminded of this with one child I have had the joy of getting to know, whose nickname is Sonic. He is an absolute fireball, and his energy is infectious. The first time I met him, I was taken by surprise because, when we hear about a child from Make-A-Wish, it's easy to imagine a kid who can barely walk or go outside, or whose condition leaves them breathless with just minimal movement. But that's not the case of every disease, and Sonic proved that. He radiates a crazy energy

that is hilarious, and when we met, he took over the scene immediately. Personally, I love goofing off, so the two of us just clicked from the start and spent the rest of the time feeding off of one another and acting like maniacs. At the end of the day, we were sitting on the bench, taking some nice, posed, smiling shots, when Sonic said he wanted to take a silly picture instead. We did, and it is now one of my favorite photos of all time. I even had it as my screen saver for a long time because I couldn't help but laugh every time I saw it, and it reminded me of the kind of person I want to be: someone who, like Sonic, lives in the moment and just enjoys the gift of being alive. That relationship has absolutely changed me and made me better.

They all make me better, in one way or another. But I think the longest-lasting relationship I've had was with Cody, as I watched him grow from a teenager to a young man, loving life and coaching soccer even while he bravely battled cancer. Sadly, Cody died recently, and the sting of his death is still very fresh for me because I didn't just know him as a sick boy I cared about but as a friend I was rooting for. In the days following Cody's funeral, his family and friends left messages on my Facebook page talking about how much he meant to them and how much he will be missed. I was deeply touched that they would include me in those memorials to him, because it gave me a chance to really understand what an impact he was able to have on other people. Even though he was so ill and somewhat limited in what he could do, even though his life was so very short, he made a lasting difference in the lives of others.

In reading those shared thoughts and in talking with Cody's dad, I felt that Cody was still affecting me, still changing me, and still making me better as his memory challenged me with this thought: if one teenager battling cancer can touch so many lives, how much more can the rest of us be doing?

IT'S ALL ABOUT ATTITUDE

Danica Patrick

Racing isn't just about speed—it's also about attitude.

You have to bring a certain mental toughness to the track so that you

aren't just trying to move faster than your competitors, but that you also

actually love the feel of the car and the road, feel a passion

for racing, and (if necessary) feel tough enough to stare down

the other drivers in a game of who's got more nerve.

Because of this, I can think of no better way to start a race than by meeting with wish children and watching the courage and joy that they bring to every moment of life. Those kids have an attitude that is impossible to fully explain—and impossible to forget.

It is a huge honor when a child has a desire to meet you. I am always curious as to what it was I might have said or done that they saw on TV or read in an interview that made them choose a meeting with me. It seems that if I can figure out what appealed to them, I can tailor our time together to really determine what will excite, encourage, or inspire the child most. Do they cheer for me when they watch races at home? Do they have models of my car that they play with? It's humbling because you don't always feel that the things you do in your life could actually strike someone else as special or unique or inspiring.

Sometimes the children and their families seem a little shy, and then we have to go through kind of a Q&A while I try to get them to loosen up and start talking so everyone can feel comfortable and relax. That was something I had to learn through experience, actually. With the first few wishes I did, I wasn't exactly sure how to break the ice, but eventually I learned that if I throw them a few softball questions they can answer without thinking, they start to feel that this isn't so intimidating after all. Then we can start having a more real conversation. It's something you have to be careful about, though. I never want to casually ask the most basic question of "How are you?" because what is the child supposed to say? "Well, I'm sick"? The one subject I absolutely try to avoid (unless they bring it up first) is their illness. The child's medical situation probably dominates every other aspect of his or her life, so I am determined that their wish day is going to be different. I never want to put a kid's struggle front and center instead of focusing on the stuff that they really want to focus on—the stuff that makes them a normal kid. In the end, it seems like most of what the kids like to talk about is the stuff that every other kid wants to talk about. I always ask about their favorite colors or games they play at sleepovers with their friends. What are their hobbies? Do they like to paint their nails? What are their favorite subjects in school?

The kids themselves almost never bring up their illnesses, either, and that's something else that impresses me about their attitudes: in no way do these children define themselves by their conditions. Instead of being dragged down or held back by their challenges, they push past them, and they understand intuitively that they are so, so much more than just their medical history. I have had the opportunity to meet with a number of incredible children over the years and I have loved every one of them, but I think two of the most recent wishes maybe do the best job of illustrating the incredible attitude these kids model for me.

The first was with eight-year-old Stephanie from New Hampshire. She had been living with Ewing's sarcoma, which is a form of bone cancer. We were able to arrange for a meeting closer to home so that she would be more comfortable. It was great to get to spend time with her at the motor speedway for the Sylvania 300 in September 2013. Stephanie was as shy as can be but looked absolutely precious in her pink T-shirt! We sat and talked for quite a while, and it was clear that she is a young lady who understands that being "girlie" doesn't mean you can't be tough, which is exactly what I believe. After we discussed it for a bit, I showed her several pairs of racing shoes and she picked out the ones she wanted me to wear for the race.

I loved how that girl had so much strength behind that sweet face. You can't be a wimp and fight a painful disease such as bone cancer. It made me so happy that I could go out and compete on the track wearing something that Stephanie had picked out; it was like she was my fashion consultant for the event, helping me look good *and* tough! Going into the race and knowing that there was a little girl and her family watching me who were facing far more serious odds than just forty-two other drivers in fast cars helped me clear my mind of distractions and worries. Their presence at that race reminded me to be grateful for the life I have, the career I love, and the strength and support of my friends, family, and fans.

Three weeks later, I got the chance to meet with Ethan, a six-year-old from Tennessee with a cerebral cyst that developed into progressive end-stage spina bifida with medullary dysfunction . . . but to listen to him crack jokes and confidently announce his ambitions you'd never know he was facing something serious. He said for his wish that he would like to take me on a date. I told him he might have to take on my boyfriend in order to do that, and Ethan right away volunteered to race him.

Ethan is one of those kids with the ability to make friends wherever they go. By the time I got to meet up with him at my motor coach, he was already best friends with half the people who work for his local Make-A-Wish office and at the track. His whole family was extremely warm and friendly. We definitely didn't need any kind of a warm-up period to get them comfortable and talking. Ethan seemed right at home from the get-go and was cracking everyone up. He brought a bunch of stuff for me to sign and, of course, I was totally happy to do so. Who can turn down such a big fan? He even pointed out that I might be able to fit into one of his jackets (I'm pretty short—only 5'2"), so I squeezed into it and we all had a good laugh about that. I had a goodie bag ready for him that included a die-cast version of my regular green GoDaddy car and my pink Breast Cancer Awareness Month car. He was pretty excited about those, but I think he was most excited about something he had brought from home. His mother had made a special shirt for him to wear to our meeting that said I LOVE DANICA. I signed that shirt right in the middle of the heart and told him I loved him, too.

That meeting put me in the best mood because Ethan's incredible attitude was so contagious. How can I possibly feel down or upset about something when I see someone so young tackling life with a huge grin and a whole lot of laughter?

All those wish kids are such a great reminder to me of how we adults sometimes get the world turned upside down. We tend to worry about everything that could go wrong or about what hasn't turned out exactly the way we want it to or about all of the terrible things in the world. These kids are *staring down* some of the most terrible things in the world, but they never seem to dwell on that. Instead, they go through their treatments and the pain of their conditions and do whatever they have to do, but they don't let the day's stress crowd out the day's excitement. With most of them, if it weren't for the fact that you can sometimes see evidence of their illness on their bodies, you would never know that they are facing any kind of serious medical condition. They are happy-go-lucky, happy to be there, to meet you, to see the race, and receive goodies and take photos. They are just happy to be alive in that moment. It is pretty powerful.

So when people ask me if I'm okay with doing a wish just ahead of a race, I tell them I can't think of a better time to do it. I understand that some athletes want to spend that time getting into competition mode, but for me, those meetings help get my mind exactly where I need it to be. They give my attitude a tune-up, if necessary, and they give me a real-life example of true toughness just when I need it most. I hope "my" wish kids know that just like they're racing right alongside me when I take the track, I'm fighting right alongside them as they face their illness with incredible courage and strength.

A TEAM RESPONSIBILITY

The New England Patriots

Editor's note: Since the New England Patriots honor all wish requests as a team, they asked that their story be shared in the third person, representing all the players, coaches, staff, and management who make these wishes possible.

Four-year-old Madeline is a tiny girl. When she was only two months old, her parents noticed a purple tumor on her skin; medical tests revealed several others developing. It turned out that Maddie was suffering from acute myeloid leukemia (AML), and it was unresponsive to normal treatments. She underwent two experimental chemotherapies, as well as a radiation treatment that had never been tried on a patient so small. Nearly 90 percent of the other babies who were being treated in her cancer ward passed away, but Maddie held on. Her pituitary gland, which controls the production and release of hormones in the body, was damaged during her treatment; as a result, Maddie is much smaller than the average four-year-old and has to take growth hormones in order to restart her body's normal childhood development. Most of Maddie's last two years have been spent in the hospital as she combats her cancer. Recently, she received a bone marrow transplant—and a wish.

Even though her family lives in Washington State, Madeline is a huge fan of New England Patriots quarterback Tom Brady and couldn't think of anything she'd rather do than meet him. Her family flew to the East Coast and visited the stadium during the Patriots' pregame warm-up; Maddie was decked out in a Brady jersey—hair braided, eyes bright, ready to go. And when she finally got to meet her hero, she squealed breathlessly, "I've been following you my *whole life*!"

Joining Maddie and her family that day were three other wish children and their families. Together they all watched, cheered, laughed, and traded stories as they talked with one another before going to watch their favorite team. As a welcome, each child was shown to his or her own locker in the locker room, each of which was stocked with a jersey, a football, and gifts from the Kraft family, which owns the Pats. Then, with all their gear in tow, they headed out to the field to meet the players. One of the boys spotted Patriots wide receiver Brandon Lloyd at a distance and called out his name. Lloyd turned, flashed a huge grin, and gave the kid a peace sign. "Brandon Lloyd just talked to me!" the boy exclaimed.

Following practice, Tom Brady came over first, to meet the children and give them a little time to talk with him one-on-one. "How tall are you?" one of the boys asked.

"I'm six feet, four inches," Brady told him, " . . . and a half."

Another boy piped up. "Which was your favorite Super Bowl?"

Brady thought a moment and then answered, "How do you pick? I still have some fingers that need rings . . . so maybe one of those in the future!"

There was a request that Brady pose the way he did during the now-famous "Tuck Rule" game back in 2002, which ended up causing a rule change in the NFL. Brady obliged, as well as every other photo op, question, or suggestions of goofiness that came his way from the children and their families. He threw passes to the kids, as well; the father of Frankie, one of the wish children, caught the ball and then

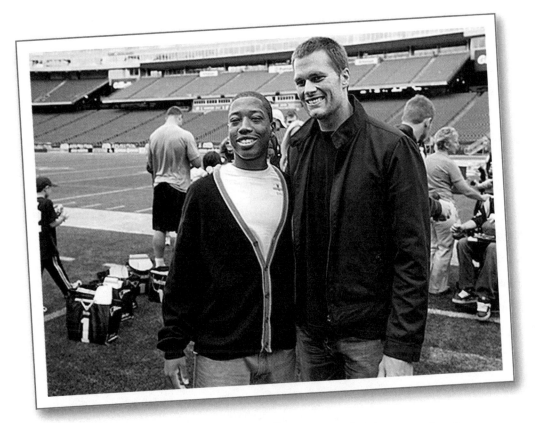

shook his head: "I just caught a pass from Tom Brady. My life is complete."

One of the boys, who was also from Washington, took off his Pats hat and showed it to Brady. "This hat has been really important to me. I got it the first time I lost all my hair from chemo," he explained. "It's been really good for me during the regular season—I had some really good luck with it. But not so much during the play-offs."

Brady laughed and asked, "Will you let me sign the hat? A bunch of other guys will want to sign this one for you, too." Then he waved his arm and the rest of the team came over, signing things for the kids, posing for pictures, and answering questions. Tight end Rob Gronkowski, who is famous for his ferocious spikes, taught the kids how to spike the ball like he does during games. Brady also signed the cast on little Maddie's arm, which she had recently broken.

As the visit was wrapping up, Maddie's mom gave her a nudge and reminded her, "You said that if you got to meet Tom Brady, you wanted to tell him something."

Brady, Patriots stocking cap on his head, kneeled down so he could be eye level with the little girl. "What was it you wanted to say?"

Maddie blushed and tucked her chin toward her chest. Then, with a knuckle in her mouth, she flashed a coy little smile and said, simply, "Hubba-hubba!"

The six-foot-four-and-a-half-inch quarterback grinned. "You're going to make *me* blush!"

Wishes are part of the New England Patriots' DNA. When Robert Kraft purchased the New England Patriots franchise in 1994, he reworked several points of the team's contracts, including a provision regarding each team member's responsibility to

charitable organizations. "What you do off the field is as important as what you do on it," said Kraft, which is why all players must make a minimum of ten appearances each year for causes other than football or product endorsements. It can be granting wishes, working with a shelter, or spending time taking part in a youth outreach program, so long as it is giving back to the community in some way.

The service clause is very near to Mr. Kraft's heart for two reasons. The first is that his late wife of forty-eight years, Myra, was an extraordinary volunteer who dedicated her life to philanthropic work. The second reason is because of the example set by Mr. Kraft's own father. "I grew up in a humble home, financially, and went to school on scholarships," he recalled. "My father left me an ethical will in which he said that getting a good name is more valuable than any material means and that every generation has to earn it for itself. He said to make sure that when you go to bed at night, people are richer emotionally for having known you."

"Every wish I go to is extraordinary," Mr. Kraft said, explaining why wish granting is so much more impactful to him than simply making a monetary donation to a foundation. "You don't get the same impact doing that as you do helping certain grassroots organizations and families. You really change people's lives. When you give a check, it's kind of amorphous. When you do something with Make-A-Wish, you know you're going to brighten the day of a child who's been dealt a bad hand and has tremendous obstacles to overcome. And when you see the pure joy on the faces of those young people, it really makes you feel better and makes you want to do more to help. Money can't buy that feeling."

Mr. Kraft said that interacting with children is important for the team, too:

"A lot of those young men come from backgrounds where they were recipients and now they get to be a donor and get the great feeling that comes from doing philanthropic work." When players find out they've been specifically requested for a wish, "it makes [them] feel a sense of self-worth. It makes their self-esteem go up."

The evidence for that is clear in the response from the team whenever Make-A-Wish reaches out to them with a request. "I don't think we've ever had a player decline a wish," he said. "It might be the only charity for which that's true. And we've had an eclectic mix of requests: Tedy Bruschi, Wes Welker, Randy Moss. With Bethel Johnson, I think it made *his* day to know someone had wished to meet him! And then he was able to have a great impact on a twelve-year-old boy." Mr. Kraft laughed, recalling one wish in particular: "Last year there was a sixteen-year-old boy from Maine whose wish was to meet a New England Patriots cheerleader. He ended up spending time with the entire squad!"

For the Kraft family, facilitating wishes is an essential part of their identity. "Some of the greatest experiences we've had as a family have been with Make-A-Wish kids," Mr. Kraft said. "We've benefited so much from seeing the joy, and the families are so grateful. For us, it's an easy thing to do. It's easy to support because it's just so good."

Recently, the Kraft family was honored for their tremendous work with and support for Make-A-Wish, and as part of the celebration, they invited a young man battling cancer to join them for the event. Mr. Kraft called him up on stage and then gifted him with a personalized, signed football, inviting him to attend a Patriot's game as part of his wish. It was a huge surprise that elicited an even bigger grin from the otherwise shy boy. But the evening wasn't over with that. From the back of the room came none other than Rob Gronkowski, the boy's favorite player. In front of the entire banquet room, "Gronk" offered a lesson on how to spike the ball, which his starstruck fan did a little timidly at first, then with more gusto. Gronk followed suit with a particularly fierce spike, and the room erupted in applause. The sheer joy on everyone's face—from Mr. Kraft's to Gronk's to the boy's—was apparent. There wasn't a dry eye in the room . . . and the wish hadn't even officially started yet.

Mr. Kraft's second-oldest son, Dan, now serves on the board of directors for

Make-A-Wish Massachusetts and Rhode Island, a role that he says resonated tremendously with him because it opened his eyes to the unique plight of children with serious illnesses and life-threatening conditions.

"I was thrilled to be asked," Dan explained. "It is such a great honor to serve because of the mission of the foundation. The kids get removed from the natural order of being a kid. They get yanked out of baseball or dance class and put into the hospital with doctors and nurses and needles and treatments and recovery. It's just a brutal life."

The impact of the wish, he said, goes beyond just one exciting day away from the worries of their everyday life.

"I've been through the whole process and when the child gets word that the wish is going to be granted, you see the excitement, the anticipation, the buildup for the kid. Maybe it's a month or two months ahead of time—then it helps them deal with the last hospital visits or the tests, the needle-pricks. It goes with them, this anticipation, to get them through that. And it's not just the kids themselves, but you see the trickle-down effect with the parents, the siblings, the other family members. It is just such a grind on these people who are going through the ordeal. It's not just about making sure the child gets a great experience, but that it ripples through the whole family so that they get to be part of it, too."

Dan added, "You don't just see the tangible results on the day of the wish, but in the buildup to it. And it doesn't end with the wish. They build a network. In the Massachusetts and Rhode Island areas there are reunions once a year around the holidays, where wish families get together and have a party for the kids. So it's not just a onetime thing that ends. It's ongoing."

For Dan, though, one of the most meaningful results of being involved with Make-A-Wish has been the impact it has had on his children. Through witnessing wishes, attending reunions, and even meeting some wish children, his daughters sought to get involved with the foundation. Several years ago, his younger daughter decided one day after learning about a child whose wish had just been granted by the Patriots that she wanted to do something to support the work of Make-A-Wish, and she wanted to do something right away. So she decided that afternoon to have a bake sale. "She mixed up some brownies, and our neighbors bought stuff," her dad remembered. "But it was important for her because she wanted to help."

When Dan's older daughter was thirteen, she found her own way to be involved. She had an assignment to contribute to a philanthropic cause, and she set her sights on Make-A-Wish.

"She worked on what they called 'Wish Enhancement Baskets,'" her father said. "If a kid was going to a theme park, she would put together a guidebook, sunglasses—whatever would help make the trip complete. On the day the family found out the wish was going to be granted, Make-A-Wish would give her basket to the kid."

He remembered going shopping for the craft materials that she would use to make each basket and how clear it was that his daughter's heart was truly invested in the project.

"A girl was going to Hawaii, and she picked out five or six stuffed whales to give her, and industrial strength sunblock because the little girl had cancer and couldn't be in the sun too long. I could see the love and care she put into each basket. She wasn't just throwing things together; she was making little cards and taking time to draw pictures for the child."

These experiences, Dan believes, have been hugely important in helping his children gain an appreciation for their own health and, more importantly, to develop a sense of how to work with compassion for others. When his son gets a little older, Dan anticipates that he'll be just as eager to help sick children receive their wishes as his older sisters have been. At Super Bowl XXXIX, Dan's children were present for one child's big moment, when he arrived at the hotel where the Krafts were staying, having been picked up in a limousine and escorted by motorcycle cops (a detail arranged by the Kraft family) to receive tickets to the game from Mr. Robert Kraft himself.

"Dad and I presented him the tickets; the cheerleaders were there. It was a great time," Dan said. And he made sure his children were present to witness the excitement of the experience for the young boy to help reinforce to them the impact of their own efforts in helping other children's wishes come true.

The Patriots players themselves have been deeply impacted by their wish-granting experiences, too. Tedy Bruschi, for example, received a call from Make-A-Wish asking if he could grant a wish on a very short timeline for an especially ill child. The very next day, he was at the hospital where he spent several hours sitting in the ICU, playing video games with the child whose wish was to meet him. Less than a month later, the child passed away. Randy Moss was another player who stepped up to the challenge to grant a last-minute wish. Within days of being contacted by Make-A-Wish, he was showing a child with a malignant brain tumor around the stadium, introducing him to the rest of the team, taking him up to the trophy room, and giving him the time of his life. The child lost his battle with cancer just a few weeks later. Both Bruschi and Moss remarked afterward that their wishes were incredibly moving and powerful events and that they were grateful and humbled to have been a part of helping those children.

Dan remarked that a large number of players have actually thanked his father for including the community service clause in their contracts. Players like Troy Brown, Kevin Faulk, Vince Wilfork, Heath Evans, Joe Andruzzi, and others have publicly spoken about the positive impact that interactions with groups like Make-A-Wish have had on their lives.

"Make-A-Wish is one that just resonates with us," Dan said about his family and the Patriots organization. "It's hard to argue with that mission statement."

A month after she received her wish, little Maddie was still talking about it. She told everyone on the airplane about it on the way home, showing off her autographed cast. She told her pre-K classmates and her teacher from the past year, who is a cancer survivor herself.

"She'll tell anyone who'll listen," her mother, Mandy, said. Maddie also made sure her mother saved her cast after it was removed.

A large part of Maddie's joy from the day has to do with the fact that it took her mind off of the worry that usually dominates it.

"Because of her illness and all she's been through, she worries about things," her mother explained. "But that whole weekend was the first time in a long time I've seen my little girl just relax and not worry about when she had to go to the next doctor or her next appointment or receive her next daily shot."

The battle with leukemia hasn't affected Maddie's spirit.

"Maddie's first wish request was actually to meet Tom Brady and for him to take her makeup shopping." Mandy laughed. "Our family is very sports-oriented, but

Maddie is also a girly-girl." Almost every Sunday of football season since Maddie was born, the family gets together to watch the Pats play, and Maddie used to proudly don the Brady jersey from her grandfather, though now she has a very special one of her own. So even though the cosmetics-shopping-spree-with-the-quarterback part of her wish didn't pan out, Maddie was still thrilled with her wish day.

"I couldn't have imagined Tom Brady running around the football field chasing Maddie. The whole team was so down to earth, not acting like superstars but just playing with the little kids. It was wonderful," Mandy said. "The one thing I wanted for her wish was something she'd never forget and something that I, as a parent, could never provide for her. Make-A-Wish and the Patriots exceeded that far beyond what I could have imagined."

EPILOGUE

DAVID WILLIAMS

President and CEO

Make-A-Wish® America

We have all received e-mails that start, "You don't know me but . . ." or "My name is ____ and have I got an idea for you!"

Well, I received such an e-mail a couple years ago from Don Yaeger, who said he had an idea for a book and would I be open to getting together? Believe it or not, we receive our fair share of inquiries from individuals who would like to write a Make-A-Wish book or create a reality show because of the amazing stories of our wish kids and their families.

But when the author is a former *Sports Illustrated* writer with twenty-four books to his credit—eight of which have been on the *New York Times* best-seller list, it does get your attention. He just so happened to be on his way to Phoenix, which is the city where Make-A-Wish began and is home to our national headquarters. So we immediately made plans for dinner the next day at P.F. Chang's, which I would soon learn is Don's favorite restaurant.

In short, Don was amazed by how often Make-A-Wish would come up in his various conversations with sports celebrities—and not in the way you might think. The conversation was not about the impact the athlete made on the child through their wish but rather the impact the child made on the celebrity. Frankly, it was not something we had thought a lot about from a message standpoint. But for those of us who have been around wish kids for any length of time, it is absolutely true. They are inspiring. What we did not know was how inspiring they are to even world-class athletes.

So we set about picking a small group of athletes who have granted wishes over the years, and we asked them to simply tell us their story. And these are their stories. These are stories that will make you laugh as well as cry, and they represent just a small slice of what Make-A-Wish does every thirty-eight minutes each and every day.

I hope that you've enjoyed reading each story but I also want to challenge you to return to these stories again, perhaps reading a chapter and reflecting on it.

Don has donated all his fees and royalties to Make-A-Wish and has traveled extensively throughout the country interviewing athletes at all hours and locations to make this book possible. On behalf of the entire Make-A-Wish family, thank you, Don, for this amazing gift.

If after reading this book, you are inspired to learn more or get involved, go to www.wish.org to learn how.

CREDITS

All photographs are courtesy of Make-A-Wish except the following:

Page 6: Brand Jordan

Page 20: Ben Van Houten

Pages 48–53: Noah Hamilton

Page 54: Karin Prunty

Page 81: *Idaho Statesman*

Page 85: Boise State Photo Services

ABOUT MAKE-A-WISH®

Make-A-Wish grants the wishes of children with life-threatening medical conditions to enrich the human experience with hope, strength, and joy. The nonprofit was founded in 1980 after a group of law-enforcement officers granted the wish of a seven-year-old boy with leukemia and experienced the power of granting a child's heartfelt wish, firsthand. Make-A-Wish has since grown to become one of the world's leading children's charities, serving children in every community in the United States and its territories. According to a 2011 survey of health professionals who refer and treat wish children, most believe a wish-come-true can have a positive impact on the health of a child. Kids say wishes give them renewed strength to fight their illnesses, and their parents say these experiences help strengthen the entire family. With the help of generous donors and more than 25,000 volunteers nationwide, Make-A-Wish has granted more than 240,000 wishes since its inception. Visit Make-A-Wish at www.wish.org to learn more.

ABOUT MICHAEL JORDAN

Michael Jordan is one of the millions who have felt the impact of a wish, and Make-A-Wish is proud to call him our friend. He is a dedicated wish granter who has touched the lives of more than two hundred wish kids since he started granting wishes in 1988. Compassionate and deeply devoted to the mission of Make-A-Wish, Jordan is one of our greatest supporters and serves as our Chief Wish Ambassador.

"When I granted my first wish more than twenty years ago, I could not have imagined the happiness and hope I'd be able to give the inspirational wish kids I've met," Jordan said. "Make-A-Wish is a big part of who I am, and it is an honor to continue to serve as the foundation's Chief Wish Ambassador as we work to grant the wish of every eligible child."

ABOUT DON YAEGER

Don Yaeger is a nationally acclaimed inspirational speaker, longtime associate editor of *Sports Illustrated*, and author of twenty-four books, eight of which have become *New York Times* best-sellers. He began his career at the *San Antonio Light* (Texas) and also worked at *The Dallas Morning News* and *The Florida Times-Union* in Jacksonville before going to work for *Sports Illustrated*.

As an author, Don has written books with, among others, Hall of Fame running back Walter Payton, UCLA basketball coach John Wooden, baseball legends John Smoltz and Tug McGraw, and football stars Warrick Dunn and Michael Oher (featured in the movie *The Blind Side*). He teamed with Fox News anchor Brian Kilmeade to pen the 2013 best-seller *George Washington's Secret Six*, a look at the citizen spy ring that helped win the Revolutionary War.

Don left *Sports Illustrated* in 2008 to pursue a public speaking career that has allowed him to share stories learned from the greatest winners of our generation with audiences as diverse as *Fortune* 10 companies to cancer survivor groups, where he shares his personal story. More than a quarter million people have heard his discussions on "What Makes the Great Ones Great." He has also built corporate programs on lessons from great sporting franchises on building cultures of success.

Learn more at www.donyaeger.com or contact Don at don@donyaeger.com.

Don would like to dedicate his work on this book to Jeanette: Thanks for making my wish come true. ILY

HOW IT ALL STARTED

Chris's Wish

During a long nighttime stakeout, kneeling in some desert weeds in the spring of 1980, U.S. Customs agent Tommy Austin tells Arizona Department of Public Safety officer Ron Cox his problem.

His wife's friend Linda has a small son named Chris Greicius who is probably going to die of leukemia. The seven-year-old boy yearns to be a police officer, "to catch bad guys" with Austin. Running into bureaucratic hesitation at Customs, Austin asks Cox if maybe DPS can do something. "I'll rent a helicopter myself if I have to," Austin says.

Cox takes the request to DPS spokesman Allan Schmidt, who asks DPS director Ralph Milstead. He gives Schmidt carte blanche to grant Chris's wish. Soon Austin receives a call from Chris's mom saying that she doesn't think he can hang on much longer.

"None of us had any idea what we were getting into at the time," Schmidt will recall thirty years later. He draws other people in: Officer Jim Eaves will bring his patrol car, and Officer Frank Shankwitz his motorcycle, to meet the DPS helicopter flying Chris to headquarters. On April 29, Chris comes from Scottsdale Memorial Hospital to the empty lot by DPS at Lewis and 19th Avenues. There he and his parents are given a tour. That's when Lieutenant Colonel Dick Schaefer gives the boy a Smokey Bear hat and one of his own old badges, and Chris becomes Arizona's first and only honorary DPS officer.

Everyone who meets the beaming boy chewing bubble gum wants to help. At the end of the day, some of those involved meet in a spontaneous group hug and realize they don't want that day to be the end of it. They also know they don't have much time.

Two of them, Cox and Eaves, go to John's Uniforms, the business that makes all DPS uniforms, and order one in Chris's size. Employees work all night to have it ready the next day. A group of officers takes the uniform to his house, where Shankwitz sets up cones for Chris to steer his battery-powered motorcycle through to qualify for a motorcycle officer's wings.

But when they return the next day to present the wings to Chris, he's gone back into the hospital. With his DPS gifts all around him, clutching his new wings, Chris gives a last smile for the men who have done so much for him in such a short time. He passes May 2.

The Beginning of a Foundation

Officers Frank Shankwitz and Scott Stahl fly back to Illinois for the funeral; Chris is given the ceremony of a fallen fellow officer.

From the time the two officers land in Chicago to when they leave again, word spreads of their story, and they are amazed at how strangers are affected by it. They talk on the flight home of making this the beginning of something wonderful for children.

Meanwhile in Phoenix, similar discussions are taking place. At an officer's retirement party, Shankwitz talks to Kathy McMorris, the wife of a DPS officer, about creating a wish-granting organization. That summer, a group of working-class DPS officers, friends, and family gather. That meeting marks the beginning of Make-A-Wish.

The first donation is fifteen dollars, given to Shankwitz by a grocery store manager. For months, records, bills, and change are kept in envelopes carried around by founders. In November 1980 the group receives its tax-exempt status as a nonprofit organization. By the following spring the group has raised two thousand dollars and can grant its first official wish.

The First Wish Kid

Frank "Bopsy" Salazar is the first official Make-A-Wish® kid. He's seven and has leukemia—just like Chris. Shankwitz is president at the time and decides to grant Poncho ("Frank" in Spanish) "Bopsy" Salazar all three of his wishes: to be a fireman, to go to a theme park, and to ride in a hot-air balloon.

So the Phoenix Fire Department gives Bopsy an experience similar to Chris's as a police officer; he becomes a member of the Engine 9 crew. Since the first wish is also the first theme-park wish, the park's local fire department picks up the baton, taking Bopsy and his family around Southern California. Shankwitz keeps the first "wish kid art," a picture Bopsy drew him, on which he wrote, "Poncho, I got to blow the siren."

Upon returning home, Bopsy goes into the hospital. His physician, Dr. Paul Baranko, is surprised at hearing a commotion coming from the boy's room and going in to see firemen climbing in through the third-story window off the fire engine ladder! Bopsy passes that night.

Every book sold will help grant life-changing wishes.